Food Addiction, Binge Eating,

Addiction Recovery

Choose: Health, Life, and Love

(with recipes)

CR Petersen M.Ed.

Earlier editions with some of the material contained here were published under the titles: <u>Five Habits of Weight Loss Success and Self-Help for the Food Addict</u>. Also published under Avoid or Reverse Type II Diabetes.

Copyright C.R. Petersen 2018

"Addiction surrenders later freedom to choose...one can literally become disconnected from his or her own will." - **Russell M. Nelson.**

Introduction

Who is this book written for?

This book is written for food addicts and binge eaters with information applicable for almost any addict. This person may have type II diabetes, prediabetes, or neither. This is not a diet book. Some people will be able to eat more than they currently eat. This is about changing behavior and thinking. This is about changing the way you think about food, life, and health. This is about lifestyle changes and enjoying life more fully. My purpose is to help you learn new skills and change thinking and behavior---if it is needed.

For some, this will require a fundamental change in thinking, a paradigm shift. It may turn your world COMPLETELY upside down, and that just may be a good thing. For many of us, our world, or at least our health is already turned upside down. There is a term some of you may have heard, "right a boat," or something similar. Our health has been turned upside down and our goal is to *right it*, or turn it back to a way that provides more opportunity for health, wellness, and smooth sailing.

Many of you may already know or believe much of what you'll read here. You have tried some of this. This may only be an affirmation of what you already know and tools to help you organize that information and put it into action.

This book is especially for binge eaters and food addicts. While binge eating is recognized as an official diagnosable disorder, food addiction is not, though anyone with one, knows it exists.

My story

My name is Pete Petersen. I am a food addict and binge eater and like a recovering alcoholic, I'm still in recovery and will be for the rest of my life.

I have a master's in education with an emphasis in psychology. My career has been spent in this field. It is primarily from a behavioral perspective; this book has been written. As a volunteer, I also facilitate, with my wife, two addiction recovery groups. Warning! Some of this may sound or feel like a 12-step program. Also as a volunteer, I have been a lifestyle coach for the Diabetes Prevention Program for many years.

Both of my parents grew up in *The Great Depression*.

My mother's family lost many of their belongings in a flood in Montana. There was no federal assistance for such things, just neighbors, friends, and family.

Because of these experiences and probably the rationing of World War II, my mother hated to waste anything. I often heard the very wise expression: "Waste not Want not!"

I would also hear a great deal about starving children in China. I was the youngest in my family. As a young child, of average weight, my mother would often tell others to give the leftovers to me. I'm sure you can imagine that my "average weight" did not last very long.

The picture on the following page was me in about 2011. I weighed over 268 pounds, had been morbidly obese for most of 30 years and obese most of my life. There aren't many pictures of me when I was this heavy because I was so embarrassed. I did believe it was important to have some pictures taken with grandchildren. You can see part of the arm of one of my grandsons in this picture.

My oldest daughter, who is in the military and in great shape, but was not always so, has another saying: "Waste it or waist it!"

Among many wonderful gifts from my mother, was the gift of learning. She was an avid and lifelong learner. I owe a great deal to my mother for many things, including my love of learning.

My father taught me the value of hard work and persistence amidst difficulties. I am grateful to both my parents for the many lessons they have taught me.

I lost over 115 pounds within a couple of years after this picture was taken. I have been able to keep it off within a few pounds ever since. I say I was over 268 pounds because I don't know exactly

how heavy I was. I stopped weighing myself at 268 pounds and know for a time I weighed much more.

Before losing the weight, I had tried and tried, lost and gained, and tried again; it only got worse. Each time I failed, I learned something. I kept studying. I kept trying. Yes, I also gave up a few times, but then I learned more and tried again. I was motivated and afraid, very afraid for good reasons...

I was shocked at how little energy I had and how little I could do physically.

I was afraid of **Alzheimer's** (sometimes called type 3 diabetes), which runs in my family.

My initial motivator was fear. Fear of Alzheimer's, fear of the things I could not do and the health complications ahead of me.

I had decided I'd rather be run over by a truck than get Alzheimer's.

As many of you may know, motivation is not enough. It is almost never enough. I was motivated, but needed more. I needed to establish a healthy foundation, develop new healthy habits, and learn new skills.

Happily, I learned there were and are better options than getting run over by a truck. I was fortunate enough to discover and use them to change my life. Since then I have helped many lose weight and overcome addictions by coaching, facilitating, and teaching in my local community.

My primary motivators today are: Health, Life (I want to live a long, enjoyable, active, life), and Love (I want to enjoy family, grandchildren, great grandchildren, my dear wife, and friends. I want to serve, love, and help others.)

This was me in 2016

Sleep Apnea – Gone

Neuropathy – Gone

Fatty Liver - Gone

High Blood Pressure (HBP) – Gone (Dr. wants me to continue to take ½ of the smallest dose of a HBP medication to protect my kidney.)

Medication for Diabetes – Gone (totally controlled by diet and exercise) My A1C has been between 4.8 and 5.2 for the past 6 years. (A1C represents average glucose control levels over approximately 3 months.)

A bonus from The Foundation has been regularity. Something many I know, struggle with.

Asthma – Well, unfortunately, I still have asthma and it's worse when there are fires in the area and smoke in the valley. During the fires, I continue walking while wearing a mask, (usually seven days a week). I also hike with Belle (my dog and good friend) as often as I can.

When I was younger, I had chronic headaches and while I still get these, they are not as frequent or severe. After I became morbidly obese, I had excruciating pain doing even minor physical activity. This has also improved dramatically, though unfortunately it has not been eliminated.

While it is certainly still possible, I no longer fear Alzheimer's. If it comes, I expect it will be a very long time from now when the rest of me is finally falling apart.

I am now much more physically active and better able to enjoy life. I had a goal to complete a 10-mile hike with my dog, Belle. I've accomplished this. I had a goal to jump rope at a fast pace 1000 times in one session. I've done it. I had a goal, and took the 5-minute plank challenge. I built up to it -- I did it. I do not plan to ever do it again! I still plank for 2 minutes at a time, almost daily. I also love to snowshoe and hike. This last summer (2017) I fell in love with a new sport. At the age of 60, I went rock wall climbing for the first time. I have now been 4 times and each experience was exhilarating. I have been able to climb more difficult walls each time. I have a goal to climb the easy side of "The Tower" (this is the tallest rock wall West of the Mississippi) at the University of Idaho.

I didn't get from being morbidly obese, to climbing rock walls and going on long hikes with my dog overnight. I do not expect you to either. You may not want to do these types of activities or be as strict as I am, that's fine. You may want something in-between.

I still struggle and slip in some areas. Other areas are easier now. I often think of choices in terms of Poor, Good, Better, and Best. Sometimes just moving from Poor to Good or from Good to Better is good enough. It's almost always best to take baby steps. It's up to you how far you want to go or how high you want to climb.

Serious disclaimers, and who this book is not written for.

My background is behaviorism, changing behavior and thinking. I am neither a physician, nor a dietician. Some of the information contained in this book may be contrary, perhaps even the exact opposite of what is commonly taught or advised. If you have diabetes or any serious medical condition, consult your physician and/or dietician and follow their advice.

Research has shown that many people can reverse type 2 diabetes, as I have done. I have also helped many lose significant amounts of weight (as much as 100 lbs.) through the diabetes prevention program. Most people who are prediabetic can avoid diabetes and the associated complications with lifestyle changes and weight loss. There is a lot of information in this book, which is not a part of the curriculum for the diabetes prevention program and which I do not teach there.

This book is NOT written for people with type 1 diabetes. It is not written for anyone with a serious medical condition unless they are using the information from this book in close collaboration and consultation with their physician and following his or her advice.

More about this book

Research and references pertaining to this book are presented in an unusual way. You will see links to a webpage/blog which will have search links to the research. Not all the research in this field is consistent. You will be presented with sometimes conflicting information. You can

Diet, exercise, drugs, and diabetes.
http://weight-lossnewsandresearch.blogspot.com/2018/01/diet-exercise-drugs-diabetes.html
http://weight-lossnewsandresearch.blogspot.com/2018/01/diet-exercice-drugs-diabetes-news.html

review and make your own decisions. Sometimes the research articles will bring up abstracts or summaries only and you must pay (a journal, not me) if you wish to read more. Some of the links will bring up news articles or other webpages which contain opinions, some expert and some perhaps not expert.

Some of this book is graphic and blunt. It is intended to be that way. As mentioned, I am a food addict and a binge eater. I have learned to use classical conditioning to make significant changes in my life. I'll explain more about classical conditioning in the last chapter. I have reprogramed my responses to certain cues or triggers and I use those examples throughout this book. My intent is not to be judgmental. You may want to reprogram your responses in different ways. My language, examples, and metaphors are how I have reprogramed my responses to cues and triggers which in the past would have compelled me to make poor choices. If you are a food addict, binge eater (or any other type of addict), you will need to find what works for you. I hope this book will help. The lifestyle changes presented in this book will require a change in both behavior and thinking for almost anyone. Most of this information applies to any addiction and an addiction of any kind is a serious topic and should not be "sugar coated." Pun intended. My intent is to offend no-one; however, this book is not for everyone.

Much (but not all) of the information contained in this book pertains to youth as much as adults. (I present some information on intermittent fasting for those who may want to try it. I DO NOT recommend intermittent fasting for children or youth. While I use a type of intermittent fasting, I eased into it very slowly over the course of a year.)

> Baby chicks must work hard to liberate themselves from their shell. If someone tries to make it easier for them, to help them, they almost always die. It is the same for the butterfly emerging from the cocoon. The best in any of us will only emerge from hard work and struggle that stretches but does not completely overwhelm. Unfortunately, too many wish for dangerous and potentially life-threatening ease.

Some of this book is written specifically for children and youth who are now succumbing to a plethora of addictions and obesity at younger and younger ages. Type II Diabetes was called Adult Onset Diabetes when I was young; however, the name had to be changed because of the millions of youth and even children, who now have the disease. It has also been discovered that it is possible for adults to develop Type I Diabetes.

If you have an addiction of any kind, and if you want to recover and remain in recovery, you must do things differently than you have done in the past. You must do things many may even find peculiar. If you are a recovering alcoholic, you need to avoid places where alcohol is served and you may need to avoid people who drink alcohol. If you are an internet pornography addict, you may have to avoid any computer with internet access unless in a supervised, controlled setting. If that is not sufficient, you may need to avoid all computers because they have become a powerful negative cue and a window to your addiction. If you are a gambling addict, you must avoid casinos and other places, including the internet, where it is accessible. If you are a shopping addict, you'd better not have credit cards.

> "The journey isn't the vista at the end, it's the ever-changing view along the way." – Toni Sorenson
>
> "The easy path will seldom lead where you need to go." – Toni Sorenson

You may need to make even more strict changes. For any type of addiction, you need to continue with helpful systems and programs of support. You will need to do and think differently than you have in the past. If you are a food addict and/or binge eater, you too must live your life differently; however, you must eat or consume calories in some way. This

> "That which we persist in doing becomes easier, not that the task itself has become easier, but that our ability to perform it has improved." - Ralph Waldo Emerson

book is about recovery and can relate to recovery of any kind, but for the food addict and/or binge eater, this book will teach you how to live life more fully than perhaps you have ever lived before.

You may not be ready to make all the recommended changes. For some of you, according to the advice of your physician or dietician, some of these changes may not be appropriate. Take and use what is beneficial and discard the rest.

An addiction can be any compulsive behavior or habit which interferes with your best health, best self, or free will, in any aspect of life. The worst addiction in the world is the one you or someone you love, struggles with.

> "To get nowhere, follow the crowd." Paul Frank Baer (Similar quotes can be found attributed to many people; however, this is the earliest citation I was able to find.)
>
> "... better to lean into the stiff wind of opportunity than to simply hunker down and do nothing." Gordon B Hinckley

You may have noticed that some addiction recovery meetings can be filled with so much cigarette smoke, you could almost "cut it with a knife." Be very careful not to replace one addiction with another. *The Foundation* (which will be explained in the following chapters) will help. Remember, *Nature Abhors a Vacuum*. Replace addictions with healthy behaviors which fill your underlying needs.

These things I choose: Health, Life, and Love.

You may have seen this on social media:

Alcohol is a great dissolver, it dissolves:

Families

Marriages

Bank Accounts

Friendships

Employment &

Brain Cells

But it won't dissolve any problems under any circumstances.

The same can be said of almost any addiction.

This journey of recovery, towards weight loss and health, or overcoming an addiction of any kind is not easy and it's not quick. The road will be bumpier than smooth. You may not be ready for the journey, that's up to you. Many in recovery will tell you it's worth the journey, it's worth the work, and the rewards far outweigh the work and temporary discomfort. Many will happily welcome you to join them and be willing to help along the way. This journey is not a sprint. You will be more successful if you are more like the tortoise, and less like the hare.

Often, we are resigned to declining health due to increasing age. While age certainly has an impact and none of us will get out of this life alive, most of us could enjoy much better health as we advance in age were we to make different choices, and knew how… So, if you're sick and tired of being sick and tired, you might, you just might, want to try some significant changes for better health.

> "Only three things happen naturally in organizations: friction, confusion, and underperformance. Everything else requires leadership." Peter Drucker
>
> The same thing can be said of our personal lives. Only three things occur naturally: friction, confusion, and underperformance. Everything else requires effective planning, based on applicable truths, put into practice with fidelity. Greater freedom to do or have anything of real value or importance, almost always accompanies work and discipline, based on correct principles.

T2D

Is it possible to reverse type 2 (T2D) diabetes? The simple answer is "yes." However, as you will see it requires tools, knowledge, and work. Recent research has found that a healthy low-calorie diet, coupled with the foundation as outlined in this book, can help many reverse T2 diabetes and avoid associated complication. Not everyone who follows this path can or will reverse T2 diabetes, but it is possible for many and improved, even substantially improved health is possible for most.

> Can T2D be reversed? You can find articles from the links below.
>
> http://weight-lossnewsandresearch.blogspot.com/2017/12/low-calorie-diet-reverse-diabetes.html
>
> http://weight-lossnewsandresearch.blogspot.com/2017/12/reverse-diabetes.html
>
> http://weight-lossnewsandresearch.blogspot.com/2017/12/reverse-diabetes-research.html

So, what are the risks?

There are many potential and increasingly common natural consequences of poor eating and drinking habits, coupled with inactivity. Some include:

Loss of Limbs, Amputation:

http://weight-lossnewsandresearch.blogspot.com/2017/09/diabetes-and-amputation.html

http://weight-lossnewsandresearch.blogspot.com/2017/09/obesity-and-amputation.html

I had one friend who lost first one leg, then another, and soon after lost his life, all due to diabetes. He was much younger than I am now.

Alzheimer's:

http://weight-lossnewsandresearch.blogspot.com/2017/09/diabetes-and-alzheimers.html

http://weight-lossnewsandresearch.blogspot.com/2017/09/obesity-and-alzheimers.html

---

I'm also going to apologize in advance for something else. At times, this book may sound like an old-time temperance activist. I try hard not to overdo, but am passionate about this subject and hope to help when and where I can.

http://weight-lossnewsandresearch.blogspot.com/2017/12/temperance-movement.html

---

One of the advantages to self-publishing on a slim budget is the ability to make updates and republish quickly and easily. There will still be updates with editing for grammar and perhaps some additional recipes; however, the basic information will be the same as contained in this edition.

If you are reading the electronic version of this book, some of the pictures will not format correctly.

Are you at risk of diabetes and diabetic complications?

Visit this webpage for many prediabetes calculators

to learn if you are at risk:

http://weight-lossnewsandresearch.blogspot.com/2017/11/free-diabetes-risk-calculators.html http://weight-lossnewsandresearch.blogspot.com/2017/11/diabetes-amputation-blindness-risk.html

Blindness:

http://weight-lossnewsandresearch.blogspot.com/2017/09/diabetes-and-blindness.html

http://weight-lossnewsandresearch.blogspot.com/2017/09/obesity-and-blindness.html

Cancer:

http://weight-lossnewsandresearch.blogspot.com/2017/09/diabetes-and-cancer.html

http://weight-lossnewsandresearch.blogspot.com/2017/09/obesity-and-cancer.html

Charcot Foot:

http://weight-lossnewsandresearch.blogspot.com/2017/09/obesity-and-carcot-foot.html

http://weight-lossnewsandresearch.blogspot.com/2017/09/diabetes-and-carcot-foot.html

Diabetic Nephropathy: (Kidney Disease and much of your life consumed with dialysis)

http://weight-lossnewsandresearch.blogspot.com/2017/09/obesity-and-kidney-disease.html

http://weight-lossnewsandresearch.blogspot.com/2017/09/diabetes-and-kidney-disease.html

Heart Disease:

http://weight-lossnewsandresearch.blogspot.com/2017/10/heart-disease-and-diabetes.html

http://weight-lossnewsandresearch.blogspot.com/2017/10/obesity-and-heart-disease.html

Neuropathy: Weakness, numbness, and/or pain in your hands, feet, and/or legs. You may have already experienced some of this.

http://weight-lossnewsandresearch.blogspot.com/2017/10/obesity-and-neuropathy.html

http://weight-lossnewsandresearch.blogspot.com/2017/10/diabetic-neuropathy.html

"Obesity causes or exacerbates many health problems, both independently and in association with

> other diseases. It is associated with the development of type 2 diabetes mellitus, coronary heart disease (CHD), an increased incidence of certain forms of cancer, respiratory complications (obstructive sleep apnea) and osteoarthritis of large and small joints. The Build and Blood Pressure Study has shown that the adverse effects of excess weight tend to be delayed, sometimes for ten years or longer. Life-insurance data and epidemiological studies confirm that increasing degrees of overweight and obesity are important predictors of decreased longevity. In the Framingham Heart Study, the risk of death within 26 years increased by 1% for each extra pound (0.45 kg) increase in weight between the ages of 30 years and 42 years, and by 2% between the ages of 50 years and 62 years. Despite this evidence, many clinicians consider obesity to be a self-inflicted condition of little medical significance." **Obesity as a medical problem** Peter G. Kopelman. St Bartholomew's & The Royal London School of Medicine, Queen Mary & Westfield College, London E1 2AD, UK
>
> file:///C:/Users/Home/Downloads/Obesity%20as%20a%20medical%20problem.pdf

None of these issues should be taken lightly. I have personally known people, and in some cases had family members with many of these conditions.

Knowing my family history of; diabetes, Alzheimer's, cancer, high blood pressure, heart disease, and obesity I had good reason to be concerned. Diagnosed with diabetes, asthma, high blood pressures, fatty liver, depression, and experiencing partial blindness, neuropathy, almost constant pain, and sleep apnea, was no picnic. I wanted to avoid or eliminate these illnesses and disabling conditions. I was a mess!

Yes, my intention here is to "scare the crap out of you." Fear is not a great motivator! However, it is important to be informed so you can avoid unnecessary risks. It is important to know your potential default future if you do not make healthy changes. My hope though, is that you will become motivated by: Health, Life, and Love. While it is currently impossible for everyone to avoid all disabilities and diseases, most of you can reduce risk by learning new skills, and changing your thinking, responses, and behavior.

Table of Contents

Who is this book written for? p.3

My story: p.4

Serious disclaimers...who this is not be for: p.7

T2D: p.11

So, what are the risks? p.11

Section 1:   The Foundation for Healthy Sustainable Weight-Loss and Health: p. 17

   Physical and Mental Health: p. 18

    a. The Foundation: p. 21

    b. Nature Abhors a Vacuum: p. 30

    c. Food Insecurity and Cravings: p. 22

    d. Food Security: p. 32

    e. Exercise: Aerobic and Strength/Resistance: p. 41

    f. Stress Management and Sleep: p. 47

5 Habits, 5 Skills and Techniques: p. 107

Section 2:   The Five Habits: p. 117

a. Weigh Daily: p. 118

b. Breakfast: p. 120

c. Exercise: p. 127

d. Share, Help, Accountability: p. 132

e. Plan: p. 138

Section 3: The Five Tools and Skills: p. 143

a. Goals and Objectives: p. 143

b. Avoid: p. 154

c. Incompatible Behaviors: p. 161

d. Alternate Behaviors: p. 164

e. Classical Conditioning: p. 168

Putting it all Together: p. 173

Section 4: Appendix with Bonus Tools, Recipes, and Quotes: p. 178

1st Section

The Foundation for Healthy Sustainable Weight Loss & Health

Physical and Mental Health

Our health, both physical and mental-emotional, is primarily the result of three important domains.

An interaction between: 1) Behavior, Choices and Thoughts; 2) Environment, Toxins, and Stressors; 3) Biology and Genetics.

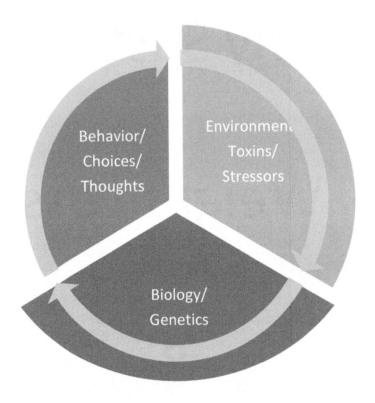

This interaction is not balanced the same for everyone. For someone born with a significant disability, syndrome, or disease, the genetics and biology may be a larger piece of the pie or personal health equation. For someone living in an extremely toxic environment such as pollution or even physical and/or mental stress, their environment may have a bigger impact. For almost everyone though; behaviors, thoughts, and choices play a part, often a much bigger part than we understand or want to admit. Many or perhaps most of us are predisposed to something we would prefer to change or avoid. That's life, we don't always get to choose the "hand we are dealt." We can, however, choose how we play the hand. We can almost always reduce risk and even change outcomes. None of us will get out of this life alive; however, we can often change the timing of our departure and our enjoyment of the journey.

Sometimes we must change or remove ourselves from a toxic environment--if possible. For almost all of us there are things we can do, changes we can make to our thoughts and behaviors, and even alterations to our environment which can have a profound effect on our health.

As you move forward on this journey, as much as possible, fix the underlying problems or causes, and not just the symptoms.

> "Don't find fault, find a remedy." Henry Ford

Your Why

To impact your health, start with your why. Why do you want to change whatever it is you want to change?

When you write **your** why; consider three angles for why you want to lose weight, or overcome an addiction? (You may also think of your "why" as your "purpose" or "reason".)

> Note: It is wise to be resourceful, to save, repair and reuse. It is never wise to eat to excess. It is never wise to consume crap or pour anything but proper fuel into an engine. This includes the marvelous engine and system that powers our mind and body and makes it possible for us to think and do.
>
> "If you don't take care of this the most magnificent machine that you will ever be given...where are you going to live?" — Karyn Calabrese

1) Is there a short-term benefit (Incentive)?

2) A long-term benefit (Reason)? (May not be, but perhaps something associated with: Health, Life, or Love?)

3) Is there something you want to avoid? (What may be your default future if you do not change? What might you fear?)

There is benefit in considering, documenting, and posting, all three. <u>Incentives</u> tend to be short-term and lack as much depth as a <u>Reason</u>. For example: Losing weight for a wedding or a vacation, is often to look good for pictures, family, and friends. New clothing, or a simple reward can provide incentive, but is not as lasting, durable, or as resilient a motivator as, Health, Life, or Love-- all long-term reasons. There is a great benefit from incentives or short-term rewards, but long-term reasons will help you better maintain weight loss, health, and recovery, over time.

> "Some things matter, some things don't. Some things last, most things won't." author

Write down at least one short term benefit or reward (incentive) one long term benefit (reason) and one thing you want to avoid by making this change. Post these three by: writing a word, finding or drawing a picture, or making a collage. Place these on the wall, or somewhere you will see them daily. Revise or change them at least every three months to keep them in your thoughts and as reminders for your motivation. Posting these become cues or triggers to help remind you to do or change, as you have planned.

When I first started losing weight I had learned the basics of the skills and habits which will be explained in this book. I had also begun to practice *The Foundation* but didn't understand how important *The Foundation* was until later.

THE FOUNDATION

```
         Stress
       Management
         Sleep

    Exercise: Aerobic
          and
    Strength/Resistance

        Food Security
```

    The earlier you establish The Foundation, daily; the healthier you will be, the clearer your mind will be, and the calmer you will be. The Foundation helps clear the mind, reduce anxiety, and energize the mind and body. For the next three chapters of the foundation, we'll start at the base and work our way up.

Food Insecurity and Cravings

I had a friend from college who tried to live on a diet of mostly macaroni and cheese and ended up having vitamin shots to restore health. This decidedly unhealthy diet, not too uncommon for many college students and far too many children, caused ill health and food insecurity. Fortunately, he has changed his ways and is now very healthy.

Millions of people around the world are both *food insecure and obese* – even morbidly obese... to include children. How is this possible? How can you be *food insecure and obese*??? You will be *food insecure* if your mind and body are missing needed nutrients. Even if you ate five gallons (that may not even be possible and could be deadly) of macaroni and cheese (and things like it) every day and nothing else, you would be *food insecure.*

CRAVINGS

Food and beverage cravings (unhealthy) come from four primary sources...

Note: Food and beverage cravings **are not** the same as physical hunger.

Food and beverage (unhealthy) cravings; drive us -- compel us -- urge us, to eat and drink, whether we are hungry or not, and whether we need additional nutrition or not.

Cravings (unhealthy) come from:

1) Food Insecurity (Not getting the nutrients our mind and body need on a daily or almost daily basis)

Myth Buster: For most people it is much cheaper to eat healthy than to eat crap.

2) Crap (if you eat or drink crap, you will crave crap)

3) Emotional Distress

#4) Habitual responses to cues, triggers, and stimuli

I'll address all four in this book.

The Human is the only animal capable of purposely and planfully, reprograming how we react to stimuli, cues, and triggers (to include crap/poison).

Before continuing, I want to explain a little more on what constitutes crap. When I think and talk about the range of what we can consume from Poor to Good to Better and then Best, everything that falls into the Poor category is what I consider crap. I have also reprogramed or reconditioned myself to associate poor eating and drinking choices with crap (manure) or poison. This association helps me avoid unhealthy food and drink. It is my practical application of Classical Conditioning.

Manure (crap)

Poison symbol

Here's a partial list of what falls under the category of crap or what I have trained myself to think of as poison.

Anything you consume that stresses your mind or body or causes disease (dis-ease) may be considered poison. In-fact, Merriam-Webster's definition suggests; in addition to causing death, poison as something that "impairs or injures an organism". Of course, due to allergies, there are also foods which constitute poison (or something you must avoid) individually. For example: Many people have life threatening peanut allergies. Though not life threatening, MSG can make me very ill. Most of the following foods and beverages raise blood sugar quickly and have little to no nutritional value. Some provide excessive stimulation to, or depress the nervous system. An insult or injury to one body system is rarely isolated to that system alone. There are almost always ripple effects throughout the mind and body.

Almost any recovering addict will have strong feelings, as do I, about the substance or object of their addiction.

Sodas (even diet)

Highly caffeinated beverages

High fructose corn syrup & sugar

White flour (most white flour, though it is possible to get whole grain and healthy white flour)

White rice

Noodles and pasta (most pasta, there are healthy options)

White bread (most, there are some exceptions)

Pastries, cakes & most cookies

Cold breakfast cereal (most, there are some exceptions)

Alcohol, tobacco, and some drugs

Energy drinks

ETC.

When blood sugar rises rapidly (due to the consumption of simple carbohydrates, sugars, or high fructose corn syrup) and then quickly and precipitously drops ("what goes up must come down") a craving and sometimes a partial system crash will result. This is like almost any addictive reaction. The same is true for rapid over stimulation due to the consumption of a stimulant, such as caffeine, energy drinks, and many drugs.

Of course, many may ask themselves, "what's the chance?" For me, it's really a matter of how many things I want to line up in my favor and how many things I want against my health and the ability to enjoy life, family, and friends, for an extended life.

While the mechanism is not exactly the same with artificial sweeteners, research has demonstrated that high concentrations of a sweet taste triggers our taste buds (that's a

---

White rice and diabetes

http://weight-lossnewsandresearch.blogspot.com/2018/01/what-rice-diabetes.html

Caffeine psychosis

http://weight-lossnewsandresearch.blogspot.com/2018/01/caffeine-psychosis.html

---

"no brainer" otherwise why would anyone eat or drink them) and causes cravings for more sweet taste, often ending in our consumption of other forms of "crap." Many artificial sweeteners can also be harmful.

Including a natural sweetener with foods when needed, is almost always safer and a healthier choice. When you get used to the natural good taste of many foods, herbs, and spices, you may find you have no need or less need for additional sweeteners.

150 years ago, for most children, one piece of candy a year was an incredible treat. I'm fine if it's rare. Today it's all too common. Crap is provided as comfort food whenever many children are in distress. We are now paying the price in physical and mental health. Too many people have learned to eat crap every time they are stressed, which adds even more stress to both mind and body. Think of the term *comfort food*. What do

---

Sugar contributes significantly to Obesity

http://weight-lossnewsandresearch.blogspot.com/2018/01/sugar-and-obesity.html

Obesity contributes significantly to Diabetes

http://weight-lossnewsandresearch.blogspot.com/2018/01/obesity-and-diabetes.html

---

you consider *comfort food*? For most of us, it is almost always crap. So many of us have learned to eat crap when we are under emotional distress. There are healthier ways to respond to stress and while it may take time, you can retrain yourself to respond or react in healthier ways when distressed. For many youth and adults, crap can have a huge impact on mental health.

Alcohol, and some other substances are depressants,

When children grow up eating healthy with very limited or no crap, they are more likely to be in-tune to natural, healthy cravings.

There is another huge problem with crap. If you eat crap, you're gunna feel like crap--if not today--eventually. And no pill will ever completely fix it. **_Ultimately, there is simply no getting around the Law of the Harvest!_**

---

and as such, depress our ability to be reflective, causing us to be more reactive. I know there are frequent articles about the benefits of some types of alcohol (as well as many of the other items on the list) even in moderate amounts; however, the dangers are not worth the potential benefits. **Any** of the potential benefits can be found in more healthy alternatives. The dangers are overwhelming; even in small amounts. If you want more information you can go here:

http://weight-lossnewsandresearch.blogspot.com/2017/08/dangers-of-alcohol.html

Alcohol is a dangerous trap for anyone trying to overcome any addiction. I'll explain this further in a later section.

Many years ago, when I was a Children and Family Therapist a colleague of mine, who was a recovering alcoholic and an addiction recovery counselor, used to say that drinking was, "suicide by the installment plan." The same can be said of many addictions.

One of my most successful class members, who lost 14% of her body weight, drinks in moderation. However, she learned there were limits in certain situations. If she passed those very moderate limits, she lost control. I must admit I have some particularly strong feelings about alcohol, above and beyond what I will explain later in the book. I have often seen the devastation of alcohol in addiction recovery groups, as a board member then chair of the board of directors for a center assisting victims of domestic violence, as a member of the Governor's Coordinating Council for Families and Children, and then a member of the executive committee. I spent seven years supervising child protection. I have seen and worked with the victims of alcoholism and drug addiction. My heart goes out to everyone involved.

http://weight-lossnewsandresearch.blogspot.com/2017/11/alcohol-cancer.html

http://weight-lossnewsandresearch.blogspot.com/2017/11/alcohol-dementia.html

COST OF CRAP

> http://weight-lossnewsandresearch.blogspot.com/2017/11/alcohol-related-death.html

Some of the crap you may consume is expensive, some is cheap, and some may even be free; but...

There is always a high cost:

1. Higher medical bills.

2. Loss of or reduction in enjoyment in whatever you are doing.

3. Loss of productivity at home and work.

4. Loss of work time, though illness.

5. Shortened life expectancy.

6. Crappy quality of life… which may include loss of sight, limbs, and open sores.

7. Clouded mind, difficulty thinking. (This is sometimes caused by low blood sugar and depression.)

8. Negative impact on relationships and time spent together. (Reducing or eliminating crap, plus establishing the foundation can extend your life and provide more time to build relationships in enjoyable, active ways.)

> Marijuana is becoming legal in many parts of the world. I won't go into a big discussion here, but encourage you to read some of the research, if only the abstracts, which are usually enough to understand the basic findings.
>
> http://weight-lossnewsandresearch.blogspot.com/2018/01/marijuana-psychosis.html
>
> http://weight-lossnewsandresearch.blogspot.com/2018/01/marijuana-schizophrenia.html
>
> http://weight-lossnewsandresearch.blogspot.com/2018/01/marijuana-and-relationships.html
>
> http://weight-lossnewsandresearch.blogspot.com/2018/01/marijuana-driving-impairment.html
>
> http://weight-lossnewsandresearch.blogspot.com/2018/01/marijuana-brain-damage.html
>
> http://weight-lossnewsandresearch.blogspot.com/2018/01/marijuana-poisoning.html
>
> http://weight-lossnewsandresearch.blogspot.com/2018/01/marijuana-and-pregnancy.html

AND…

You feel constantly compelled to eat more crap, which costs more.

> "What win I, if I gain the thing I seek?
>
> A dream, a breath, a froth of fleeting joy.
>
> Who buys a minute's mirth to wail a week?
>
> Or sells eternity to get a toy?" Shakespeare

Some people seem to do well, balancing crap and better eating. Some can straddle the fence (I cannot) but if you live long enough, consuming crap will catch up with anyone.

For most of us, though, including me, we simply cannot have one foot in crap and the other in health. (I must admit that my left big toe steps in crap on occasion, but it is rare.)

> "If you keep on eating unhealthy food, then no matter how many weight loss tips you follow, you are likely to retain weight and become obese. If only you start eating healthy food, you will be pleasantly surprised how easy it is to lose weight." Subodh Gupta, <u>7 Habits of Skinny Women</u>
>
> "Those who have one foot in the canoe, and one foot on the shore, are going to fall into the river." – Tuscarora
>
> "Sorry, there's no magic bullet. You gotta eat healthy and live healthy to be healthy and look healthy. End of story." — Morgan Spurlock, <u>Don't Eat This Book</u>

Unfortunately, you must also be a crap detective.

There are many products which appear to be healthy, but contain crap. Read the labels and look for hidden crap. Three things to be especially aware of, are:

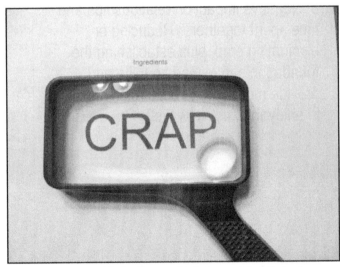

1) Serving Size: Quite often, you will see calories listed and it won't look like much. Then, even though the bag or package is quite small, when you look at the number of servings it will say 2 or 3 servings. If you eat everything in the bag you must multiply the calories and fat listed, by the number of servings.

> As a "rule of thumb," fats from: fruit (e.g. avocado

2) The order of ingredients: Quite often you'll look at a food label and when you look at the first ingredient, you think, "that looks healthy." As you continue down the list of ingredients you might see sugar listed, then high fructose corn syrup, then perhaps another type of sugar listed. It gives the impression that there really isn't much crap, but in fact, there is a lot of crap. For many healthy foods, such as whole wheat bread, you may see sugar on the list. While it would be better to avoid sugar, quite often it can be very difficult to avoid completely. You need to be especially wary, when you see one type of crap listed after another.

> and olives), nuts & seeds, and fish (most) are healthier choices. However, while you are ok to eat a little more fat than recommended if it's a healthy fat, it should still be limited. I typically average about 55 grams of fat per day when I'm maintaining and about 33 grams per day when I am losing weight. If you are morbidly obese, you will want to start at around 55 grams per day and slowly reduce the grams of fat as you lose weight. Don't average below 33. I average on a weekly basis.

3) Ingredients you can't, or have difficulty pronouncing. Be wary of ingredients with long, scientific sounding names.

> "The center [of the supermarket] is for boxed, frozen, processed, made-to-sit-on-your-shelf-for-months food. You have to ask yourself, "If this food is designed to sit in a box for months and months, what is it doing inside my body?" Nothing good, that's for sure." — Morgan Spurlock, <u>Don't Eat This Book</u>

REMEMBER

It's about both:

Crowding Out: inserting food security in your life.

And

Cutting out: eliminating the crap.

Over time you can come to think of food as fuel, which is, or should be, its primary purpose. You will **eat to live instead of living to eat**. This does not mean you

> You may want to make a sign and post it where you can see it: I Do Not Eat or Drink Crap! Remind yourself of this when tempted.

can't enjoy your food; you can and hopefully will as I do. However, food is neither my primary enjoyment nor comfort for life's many stresses.

NATURE ABHORS A VACUUME

Forgive me, this is just an example of my odd humor. What this means is: nature abhors a void, and will always seek to fill it.

Forget about the old starvation diet. I use intermittent fasting quite frequently and you **MAY** want to try it too, as I'll describe later. Done the right way, this can be a great strategy for binge eaters; however, starvation is NEVER the way to go. It's not healthy, it's not smart, and it's a terrible long-term solution because it NEVER works long term. Eventually, your health will plummet and you will likely die sooner if you do not learn to make healthier lifelong choices.

"Hunger and self-control do not go hand in hand." Kathy Freston

There are many high fiber foods which provide great health benefits and very low calories.

Remember: "Nature abhors a vacuum." If you eliminate one thing, you must replace it with something else. Choose something healthy. If you do not; something, often something less healthy, will find its way to fill the void. The Foundation can help you develop better self-control and self-efficacy, which can in turn help you develop and exercise better control in **all** aspects of your life. This Foundation will help you think more clearly and help you be more reflective and less reactive in day to day decisions. The Foundation, plus the habits and skills discussed later, will help you fill the void created by the unhealthy habits and choices you leave behind.

"The reason fiber helps us control our weight is that it fills the belly yet yields few calories since fiber is for the most part, not something that we can digest." Kathy Freston

"Whole foods like grains and beans release their sugar very, very slowly because of the fiber in them they don't give you a sugar rush. They feed your cells as needed and as a result, you have loads of stable energy that powers you through the day." Kathy Freston

Some changes may need to be immediate (according to the direction of your physician) for individual reasons. Most of the changes discussed here can and should be taken a step at a time. When I teach classes, I tell everyone right at the beginning that we will take baby steps and not to worry about trying to make huge changes quickly. We do better starting off setting small reasonable goals, which require some work and stretching, but are not overwhelming.

When I was young we lived just outside the city limits and had enough land to keep a few farm animals. Unfortunately, the barn and corral were at the lowest point on the property. In early spring, the manure would be up to my knees. I would wear irrigation boots to feed animals and enter the barn to milk after washing the udder of the cow. (We had a small milk pasteurizer for additional sanitation.) One day, a family we knew, came over with their pickup to get a load of manure for their garden. After their pickup was loaded, one of their sons who was about a year younger than me decided he didn't want to slowly and laboriously pull his feet, one at a time, out of the manure and walk to the fence and climb out. He  decided, instead, that he could jump the distance to the fence and be done with it. He made a great effort; however, his boots remained right where they had been and he landed face down in the corral, in the deep manure.

Sometimes our unwise inclination may be, to make quick and drastic changes without establishing a firm foundation and developing the right positive habits and skills. Sometimes, slow and steady, establishing a firm foundation, really does win the race. It can also be very helpful to have someone extend a hand to help pull you out of the crap.

THE FOUNDATION: LEVEL 1, FOOD SECURITY

Whole Grains
(e.g.
Rolled Oats,
Rolled Barley, Brown Rice),
Vegetables, Fruit,
Protein (mostly plant based)
some dairy (or the nutrients
found in dairy, such as from dark
leafy green vegetables),
Legumes (e.g. beans and lentils), some Nuts and Seeds,
Healthy Fats (which can vary slightly according to individual needs).
Essential vitamins and minerals.

Most essential daily, are: whole grains, vegetables, fruit, and protein. (While I eat meat sparingly, I am not a vegetarian.) Use a wide variety of plant based protein foods, such as kidney or pinto beans, brown rice, and quinoa. I also use protein powder in smoothies. I prefer pea protein powder much of the time.

For most of us, it's important to lay The Foundation, each of the three levels, as early as possible, every day.

If you eat like this AND eliminate crap, almost anyone can save money on both food and medical bills.

And...

> http://weight-lossnewsandresearch.blogspot.com/2017/09/meat-and-cancer.html
>
> http://weight-lossnewsandresearch.blogspot.com/2017/09/meat-and-inflamation.html

While not a cure all, The Foundati

on can help, sometimes significantly, both physical and mental health. The Foundation can help reduce symptoms, prevent conditions, and make life more enjoyable. This is a picture of me walking with Belle and my granddaughter.

While preparing this book, I was speaking with someone who was ill and had an infection. I reminded her to drink lots of water. Her response was that water was boring. My response to her was that boring was lying sick in bed.

Be sure to drink plenty of clean water... but not to excess.

It can take a while to really enjoy healthy food. It took me about 2 years. It only took me about two weeks to start to feel **a lot** better, and to be able to do a lot more. Feeling better and thinking clearly was much more important to me than great tasting food.

Most of the time, I **FEEL GREAT** now! Now great nutrition tastes great! **It can for you too!**

For some with type 2 diabetes, limiting (but not eliminating) carbohydrates may be important; however, eliminating or severely limiting crap, is essential for optimal health. For a food addict or binge eater, it may actually be easier to completely eliminate crap, than to try to severely limit it. Crap includes all those simple, fast digesting carbs you should avoid like you would the plague. Don't misunderstand. Eat a well-balanced healthy diet. Limit calories and fat. Follow the advice of your physician.

> This type of eating resembles, but is not the same as a ketogenic

Remember, there is a world of difference between complex carbs, and simple carbs/crap. Combinations also matter, establishing good food security and the rest of The Foundation can help stabilize blood sugar, though if you have diabetes, you **must** continue to take measurements and follow the advice of your physician. Like sugar and high fructose corn syrup, simple carbs tend to raise blood sugar levels sometimes quickly followed by a steep and quick decline. Complex carbohydrates work much more slowly and evenly. Sometimes the emphasis on low carbohydrates is due to the lack of understanding of the difference between complex and simple carbs or crap. Eat whole grains, such as rolled oats and brown rice.

diet, which may allow much more of certain types of fats. While a ketogenic diet may benefit some with diabetes, there are some concerns about the long-term and overall health effects. While I limit fats, because I eat very healthy fats, I will often eat slightly more than recommended limits. I have also slowly transitioned to being able to use a variation of intermittent fasting.

http://weight-lossnewsandresearch.blogspot.com/2018/01/ketogenic-diet-diabetes.html

Eat beans in moderation. Eat fresh vegetables. Eat starchy vegetables such as corn, potatoes, and peas, sparingly. Eat no crap. This is much healthier for and easier on the body and mind. I moved from eating mostly crap to mostly good and better foods quite quickly. The transition to eating mostly good and best foods took about two years.

http://weight-lossnewsandresearch.blogspot.com/2017/12/complex-carbohydrates-and-diabetes.html

This can make it a bit more complicated, but some try to eat foods, with a low glycemic index.

http://weight-lossnewsandresearch.blogspot.com/2017/12/low-glycemic-index-foods.html

http://weight-lossnewsandresearch.blogspot.com/2017/12/high-glycemic-index-foods.html

Most Essential for Food Security

Start your day with 1 serving of protein, 1 serving of fruit, 2 servings of whole grains, and 2 servings of vegetables.

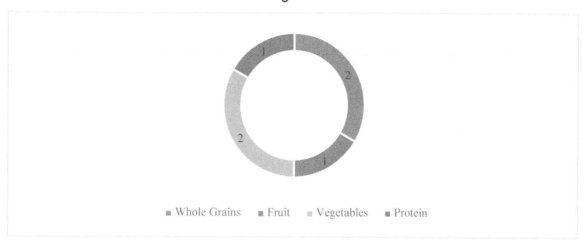

A good multivitamin and multimineral can also help. While *the foundation* is fundamental. Supplemental nutrition, (without consuming more than needed, please consult your physician) can be extremely helpful for most.

For example: some research has found that as many as 75% of all cases of autism can be avoided with the right vitamins and minerals before and during pregnancy. The prevention of other developmental disabilities can also be aided by *the foundation* and supplementation. This supplementation to *the foundation* can have a profound impact on the physical, mental, and emotional health of many.

http://weight-lossnewsandresearch.blogspot.com/2018/01/vitamins-pregnancy-autism-risk-75.html

http://weight-lossnewsandresearch.blogspot.com/2018/01/vitamins-pregnancy-autism.html

For related information, see:

http://weight-lossnewsandresearch.blogspot.com/2017/09/myplate.html

Sample Recipe:

Here's an example of what I call sneaky nutrition, something that will help establish Food Security. Make a batch, save some for breakfast and treats. This bar has something from every important food group.

You can start with a blender to mix all the ingredients except the seeds, if you are using rolled oats. If you use wheat flour or oat flour you can add everything in a bowl and use a mixer.

Full Meal Super Energy Bar

Add to a blender or large bowl:

4 large eggs

3 cups rolled oats or oat flour or whole wheat flour (You always want to blend the rolled oats if you use them.)

2 cups skim milk or cashew, almond, or soy milk

1 cup honey

2 cups no sugar added peanut butter (fresh ground is best)

2 cups zucchini (if doing this in a blender, you can add zucchini, cut into small pieces, if in a bowl and using a mixer, shred the zucchini)

Blend well. If in a bowl, mix these ingredients well.

If you do the first part in a blender, pour the mixture into a bowl and use a mixer for the rest.

1/2 cup pumpkin seed

1/2 cup sunflower seed

1/2 cup raisins

1 cup Chia seed

1 tsp baking powder

1tsp baking soda

Mix well.

Spray a large cookie sheet with spray oil

Pour all ingredients into the cookie sheet.

Put into an oven, preheated to 400 degrees.

Bake for 15 to 20 minutes. (Put kitchen knife or fork into bars to make sure it comes out clean and the bars are completely cooked. Don't overcook.)

Cut into serving sizes. Best served warm.

Now if you were to eat the whole pan (using the 3 cups rolled oats) all by yourself... which is not recommended, you would consume:

Calories: 3517 calories

Fat 180.9g

Cholesterol 755.4g

Sodium 746.6mg

Carbohydrates 636.8g (mostly complex)

Fiber 123.9g

Sugars (natural) 334.1g

Protein 154.1g

Eat just a little, then save in a refrigerator for later, or share the rest.

No added Sugar, No Butter, No Bake Cookies: Gluten Free

Pour into a large bowl:

A range of ingredients allows for you to adjust to your own taste.

3 cups rolled oats. If you need it to be gluten free, get certified gluten free rolled oats.

4-6 tablespoons Dutch baking chocolate

1/2 - 1 cup stevia

1/2 to 1 cup fresh ground peanut butter or Adams (or another no sugar added) peanut butter

1/2 to 1 cup no sugar added coconut flakes

1 tablespoon vanilla

Add to a saucepan: 3/4 to 1 cup virgin organic coconut oil (put on the stove and stir and warm slowly until hot but not boiling, then pour into the mixture above)

Mix well with wooden spoon. Compress into balls with hand and place on a cookie sheet on wax paper. Cover with the same. Put in the freezer. When frozen, move into a container for the freezer. Best served frozen.

Many of you may want a little less chocolate and a little less coconut flakes.

Note: Many recipes will contain stevia. You can and should adjust the amount of stevia to taste. While I prefer stevia, some may prefer sucralose.

As mentioned previously, I am not a vegetarian, but I eat very little meat. One of the previous research links provided articles on the association of meat and inflammation. The next important connection to understand is between inflammation and pain.

The inextricable connection between food and health has been understood for thousands of years. How is it, we seem to have forgotten this in the age of modern medicine? I'm grateful for the marvels of modern medicine, but understand it cannot forever make up for poor choices.

Many cultures and religions around the world have spoken and written on health and wellness for millennia. Here are some examples:

"When you rise in the morning, give thanks for the light, for your life, for your strength. Give thanks for your food and the joy of living. If you see no reason to give thanks, the fault lies in yourself." Tecumseh (Native American)

"To keep the body in good health is a duty otherwise we shall not be able to keep our mind strong and clear." Buddha

"The food we take daily has its effect on our psychology and character. It may be satvik, good and strengthening to the spirit; or destructive of serenity; passion-producing, rajasik; or wholly bad causing deterioration of mind and intellect and increasing inertia, tamasik." BhagavadGita Chapter VII 8-10 (Hindu)

"Let food be thy medicine and medicine be thy food." Hippocrates (Greek)

"No disease that can be treated by diet should be treated with any other means." — Maimonides (Jewish philosopher, writer, and physician, who practiced in Egypt and figured prominently and was mentioned extensively in the literature of Islamic and Arabic science.)

"Eat less you will be healthier." Hadith (Islamic)

"And it is He Who produces gardens trellised and untrellised, and date palms, and crops of different shapes and taste (it's fruits and its seeds) and olives, and pomegranates, similar (in kind) and different (in taste). Eat of their fruit when they ripen." Quran (interpretation) 6:141 (Islam)

Daniel Chapter 1:11 Then said Daniel to Melzar, whom the prince of the eunuchs had set over Daniel, Hananiah, Mishael, and Azariah,

12 Prove thy servants, I beseech thee, ten days; and let them give us pulse to eat, and water to drink.

13 Then let our countenances be looked upon before thee, and the countenance of the children that eat of the portion of the king's meat: and as thou seest, deal with thy servants.

14 So he consented to them in this matter, and proved them ten days.

15 And at the end of ten days their countenances appeared fairer and fatter in flesh than all the children which did eat the portion of the king's meat.

16 Thus Melzar took away the portion of their meat, and the wine that they should drink; and gave them pulse. (Judeo/Christian)

1st Corinthians 6:19 What? know ye not that your body is the temple of the Holy Ghost which is in you, which ye have of God, and ye are not your own? (Christian)

Doctrine and Covenants Section 89:10 And again, verily I say unto you, all wholesome herbs God hath ordained for the constitution, nature, and use of man—

11 Every herb in the season thereof, and every fruit in the season thereof; all these to be used with prudence and thanksgiving.

12 Yea, flesh also of beasts and of the fowls of the air, I, the Lord, have ordained for the use of man with thanksgiving; nevertheless, they are to be used sparingly;

13 And it is pleasing unto me that they should not be used, only in

times of winter, or of cold, or famine.

14 All grain is ordained for the use of man and of beasts, to be the staff of life, not only for man but for the beasts of the field, and the fowls of heaven, and all wild animals that run or creep on the earth;

15 And these hath God made for the use of man only in times of famine and excess of hunger.

16 All grain is good for the food of man; as also the fruit of the vine; that which yieldeth fruit, whether in the ground or above the ground—The Church of Jesus Christ of Latter-day Saints

Whether you are religious or not, sometimes the wisdom of the ages, of millennia, should not be as easily discounted as it often is.

http://weight-lossnewsandresearch.blogspot.com/2017/09/processed-meat-diabetes-heart-disease.html

http://weight-lossnewsandresearch.blogspot.com/2017/09/health-effects-of-meat-consumption.html

http://weight-lossnewsandresearch.blogspot.com/2018/01/inflammation-meat-pain.html

So many people stop learning and stasis sets in by 40. Too much hubris. Too many of us are too proud to learn from children. Too many of us are too proud to learn from the aged or the ages. Too many find a flaw or fault and disregard the rough gems in life.

THE FOUNDATION: LEVEL 2, EXERCISE

SM&S

Exercise:
Aerobic:
6-7 x per week
for at least 20 minutes.
Strength/Resistance 2-3 x per week

FOOD SECURITY

For example: Walking is sometimes called the **Super Food of Exercise**.

Resistance bands are a simple and great way to incorporate strength-resistance exercise. They can also be used sitting.

Pulling weeds can be a great way to incorporate a combination of exercises, give you a

sense of accomplishment, and burn calories at the same time.

Exercise can look a lot like play. Exercise can look a lot like just having fun.

By the way, it's OK for adults to play too. If you play with children, such as your own children or grandchildren, everyone will just think you're being a great parent or grandparent and won't think you're weird. As a grandpa, I can even get away with singing silly songs in public while walking with my 4-year-old granddaughter. And she loves it!

Exercise can look a lot like work.

Exercise can be done by almost anyone, anytime, and anywhere.

Remember, you don't have to do it all at once.

Start where you are.

Build slowly.

Consult with your doctor as needed.

Walking, playing, working, even sitting doing chair aerobics or using stretch-resistance bands or weights, can all be exercise. Do things you like doing, with people, or pets, you enjoy.

Most Essential

Start your day with:

Aerobic Exercise

Gradually build up to at least 25 minutes per day, if possible. Walking in a swimming pool can be a good way to start for some. A brisk morning walk can do wonders to clear the mind, invigorate the body, reduce anxiety, improve mood and physiology.

> Vitamin D and Diabetes
>
> http://weight-lossnewsandresearch.blogspot.com/2017/10/vitamin-d-and-

Walking is much better for the mind and body than loads of caffeine. Walking outside and collecting vitamin D (without getting too much sun) provides an added health bonus. (Use sunscreen when necessary.) If you are a heavy coffee drinker and decide to reduce or eliminate coffee you will likely have withdrawal symptoms and may want to speak with your medical provider before doing so.

diabetes.html

Coffee and cancer

http://weight-lossnewsandresearch.blogspot.com/2017/09/coffee-and-cancer.html

Diabetes, cancer, and sunlight exposure

http://weight-lossnewsandresearch.blogspot.com/2018/01/diabetes-cancer-and-sunlight-exposure.html

I do consume some caffeine from baking chocolate.

List of foods that may also help you wake up, become energized, and alert:

Apples, Apple Cider Vinegar, Avocado, Blueberries, Chia Seeds, Cinnamon, Grapefruit,

Leafy Greens, Lemon, Nuts, Oatmeal, Peppermint, Quinoa, Spinach (fresh)

If you are currently addicted to caffeine, you are likely to experience symptoms of withdrawal as/if you stop consuming caffeine.

You can find smoothies and other recipes with most of these ingredients here:

http://quickhealthymealsonabudget.blogspot.com/

AHA Recommendation

For Overall Cardiovascular Health:

- At least **30 minutes of moderate-intensity** aerobic activity at least **5 days per week for a total of 150**

    OR

- At least **25 minutes of vigorous** aerobic activity at least **3 days per week for a total of 75 minutes**; or a combination of moderate- and vigorous-intensity aerobic activity

AND

- **Moderate- to high-intensity muscle-strengthening activity** at least **2 days per week** for additional health benefits.

For Lowering Blood Pressure and Cholesterol

- An average **40 minutes of moderate- to vigorous-intensity** aerobic activity **3 or 4 times per week**

What if I can't make it to the time goal?

Something is always better than nothing!

American Heart Association Recommendations for Physical Activity in Adults

THE FOUNDATION: LEVEL 3, STRESS MANAGEMENT AND SLEEP

Stress Management and Sleep: Everyone has stress and there can be benefits from stress, for growth and developing resilience (when responded to and managed appropriately). Learn to manage and even use the right kind and level of obstacles/stress for growth and self-improvement. **Get a Good Night's Sleep.**

Exercise

Food Security

STRESS

Can make us better or bitter.

      In a sense, it's your choice…

            But that's too simple…

   Using these struggles to make us better, sometimes requires a change of attitude AND new skills, which CAN be learned and developed.

Sometimes we need help…

   Sometimes, and this is very important, we need to be the help…

> "If you want to lift yourself up, lift up someone else." - Booker T. Washington

> Remember: This book provides pages with links to related research. Some of the research may contradict other research. That's ok, if it is something you question, look deeply, investigate, try it out, and you decide what is helpful and what is not.

STRESS IS BOTH PHYSIOLOGICAL AND EMOTIONAL

Whenever anyone moves into acute or significant chronic stress there is an inner change. This change is both physical and psychological. Most of the time, when someone experiences significant stress, before they can return to or regain a state of calm and relaxation there must be a reversal--relaxation, and healing, or rejuvenation, of both the physical and psychological. There must be both a physiological and emotional restoration. Sometimes this requires a change in the way we interpret and process information and/or our expectations. Sometimes it requires healthy, usually aerobic, physical activity.

We'll talk a great deal more about some of these changes; however, some great insights are found in "The Happy Secret." Watch the video here:

http://quickhealthymealsonabudget.blogspot.com/2017/08/the-happy-secret-to-better-work-shawn.html

Try doing as suggested. Write down at least three things you are grateful for every day and sincerely thank someone every day for something. It will change your life. It may change someone else's life. It will help you reduce stress. It can help you obtain better physical and mental health.

To reduce and/or manage stress all the following can be helpful. The list is quite long, so PLEASE don't STRESS yourself out by trying to do them all at once. Pick one or two you want to work on. When they have become habit and/or you have gained the skill, pick one or two more you want to work on. Don't work on more than one or two at a time and only work on the ones you believe will be most helpful.

Like it or not, your example will almost always have a more powerful impact on your children, other children with whom you associate, or anyone else for that matter, than anything you will ever say.

> Remember when trying to help your children or others:
>
> "What you do speaks so loudly that I cannot hear what you say." - Ralph Waldo Emerson

REDUCING AND MANAGING STRESS

All of this may seem like an enormous amount of almost insurmountable work; however, if you take this in small baby steps, learn to fail forward, and pick yourself up and start again when you fall **or** fail, you will find that over time, it becomes easier and easier. You can become more efficient and able to accomplish more than you had previously thought possible.

> "People's beliefs about their abilities have a profound effect on those abilities. Ability is not a fixed property; there is huge variability in how you perform." - Albert Bandura

1. Decrease the dissonance between levels of control and expectations of control.

> "When you take the time to cleanse your physical body of accumulated stress and toxicity, you are rewarded with increased vitality and optimal health." - Debbie Ford

Dissonance refers to conflict, incongruence, or lack of agreement. One of our principle stresses in life is believing we should have control over something we do not, should not, and/or cannot control. One of our chief causes of stress comes from when we attempt to exert control where we have or should have little or none, and neglecting to control where we could and should, (quite often ourselves). Sometimes the lack of self-control fosters this perceived need to control others, things, or events outside of our control. This is an area where I personally have and at times, continue to struggle. I am prone to "tilting at windmills" (See Don Quixote *The Man of La Mancha*). Sometimes these windmills are things I can and should change and sometimes they are not and as in the *Serenity Prayer*, I occasionally have a hard time knowing the difference.

This brings me to the work on Need Achievement popularized by the psychologist David McClelland. Those with very low need achievement tend to choose very difficult tasks, so difficult that in their estimation 'no one, certainly no average person could be expected to have accomplished the task,' or they choose very easy tasks, tasks so simple 'anyone could have done it.' Either way, they can rationalize that they cannot be given credit for completing the task OR blame for failure. It's neither their fault nor their success.

On the other hand; people with a high need for achievement tend to set goals reasonable for themselves, yet stretching themselves enough to increase their own personal capacity, resilience and level of achievement. If there is an area where you feel a strong need to increase your positive influence over others, and where you are willing to pay the price in effort, read <u>Influencer, the Power to Change Anything</u> by Vitalsmarts.

While you may have influence over the behavior of others, you will not and should not attempt to have total control. One of the goals of a good parent is to teach their child good self-control. One of the ways to help children develop good self-control is to model it in yourself. Exercising good self-control will help teach your child to do the same. Setting appropriate limits for children is not the same as controlling them. Allowing and encouraging choices within those limits, even allowing them to make some mistakes which are neither illegal, immoral, nor life threatening, is an important part of the learning process. Setting appropriate and firm boundaries for children is also essential for their benefit, yourself, and society.

Let go of what you cannot or should not control. Take control of what you can and should. It will drastically reduce your stress.

> "To enjoy good health, to bring true happiness to one's family, to bring peace to all,

How to help yours, or another child, understand and correctly exercise control:

> one must first discipline and control one's own mind. If a man can control his mind he can find the way to Enlightenment, and all wisdom and virtue will naturally come to him." - Buddha

Help children understand (to the level appropriate for the child) the difference between what and where they do and do not have control. Too often children believe they are somehow to blame for your stresses. Sometimes it comes from the belief, natural for young children, that the world revolves around them and sometimes it is because of something you or others may have said; but, which was misunderstood by your child. (Unfortunately, there are some who will blame a child or anyone for their own faults and weaknesses.) As much as is appropriate for the child, help them understand what is going on when you face significant stress, but only to the degree appropriate for their developmental abilities. Partner with your children in finding solutions, e.g. hold family councils on home production and ways to save money. Discourage children from believing they are responsible beyond their level of responsibility and developmental abilities.

Blame is not constructive, neither is rationalizing. Look for ways to problem solve and/or achieve goals incrementally.

2. Increase feelings of security and certainty.

> Take responsibility and give credit where it is due.
>
> "As we make and keep commitments, even small commitments, we begin to establish an inner integrity that gives us the awareness of self-control and the courage and strength to accept more of the responsibility for our own lives. By making and keeping promises to ourselves and others, little by little, our honor becomes greater than our moods." Steven Covey
>
> Cognitive dissonance and stress:
>
> http://weight-lossnewsandresearch.blogspot.com/2017/08/cognitive-dissonance-and-stress.html

We live in a world where many search for, and at times feel it almost impossible to find security and certainty. Refugees flee from war, terror, despotic governments, economic distress, and natural disasters. Families are torn apart. Children, with or without a parent, are forced from or flee from danger and violence in their home, neighborhood, or nation. Human trafficking and slavery are huge and distressing problems in our world today, almost always with unimaginable horror. For most of these unfortunate individuals, there is little they can do to change their situations. Fortunately, there are some in the world who try to confront and stop these terrible evils and help those in need. According to the UN, approximately 40 million people are in slavery today. More than at any time in the recorded history of the world.

This slavery of which I wrote above, refers to the horrors, degradations, and deprivations, of actual physical bondage. However, millions more are in the grips of another type of bondage and the chains are often just as or almost as powerful. They too desperately need help. Sometimes these chains are initially self-inflicted and sometimes they are not. These people are our brothers and sisters, neighbors, family, and friends. Millions of people are in the awful grips of addiction with its many ugly faces. There is help, there is hope. Sometimes you can be a part of that help and hope. Many need a friend and/or family member to lift, to invite, and take the journey with them. Many need you or someone, to take them by the hand, attend a recovery meeting, and continue to support them in attendance and/or as an active mentor and friend.

If the addict is your child or teen, you <u>may</u> have additional leverage if used effectively. If there are legal issues, law enforcement and courts, have additional leverage, but no matter the circumstances, you may have influence and be able to provide support. Even if the addict will not attend, there are support groups for family and friends. These groups can help family and friends better understand their influence and boundaries, what they can and cannot do, and how to support and heal themselves. You or they may also want to read <u>Influencer</u> by VitalSmarts.

> http://weight-lossnewsandresearch.blogspot.com/2017/10/modern-slavery.html

While some situations as mentioned above, are almost hopeless, for most of us there are things we can do to help make the stress of chaos just a little easier to manage. Amidst

> "But no matter how much evil I see, I think it's important for everyone to understand that there is much more light than darkness." — Robert Uttaro, <u>To the Survivors: One Man's Journey as a Rape Crisis Counselor with True Stories of Sexual Violence</u>

the darkness, there are brilliant beacons of light in the world. Find the light whenever and wherever possible. Do what you can to be a beacon to others. As much as possible, maintain routines and schedules. This includes bed and meal times, *as much as possible*. Having a different schedule on the weekend, staying up late and staying in bed for an excessively long time disrupts the sleep cycle and makes both physical and psychological stress even worse. While it's good to sleep in once or twice a week until your body naturally awakens, it's easier on your body to maintain a consistent bed and wake time throughout the week. Even once a week after allowing yourself to sleep in, when you wake up (other than to use the restroom), get up. Routines and schedules, free your mind to think about, organize, and be creative about more important matters. This is partially due to the power of habits. Allowing ourselves to complete routine tasks almost mindlessly allows us to focus on and sometimes resolve more important issues at hand. When our schedule is chaotic, we must spend more mental energy managing our routines.

> Traditions can also create a sense of security and connection with others and with the past. As I write this I am reminded of the famous Christmas Truce of 1914 during World War 1.

Remembering and honoring traditions in even the most horrific situations can provide a bit of inner peace through the connections created: with family, friends, our own past, our family history, or the history of a group to which we belong. These connections help create a greater sense of security and personal grounding.

http://weight-lossnewsandresearch.blogspot.com/2017/09/world-war-1-christmas-truce.html

Traditions can help connect us with our roots. While some of our roots may be unpleasant, there is something positive in everyone's roots (family tree) when they are able to look back, deep and far enough. My mother had many strong German traditions around Christmas which we enjoyed and honored as a family. My wife and I have nurtured many traditions with our own family and with the many international students who have lived in our home over the years.

Family history is another way to help both children and adults connect with their roots. Children who have lost a parent through tragedy have sometimes found a connection through family history. This connection helps develop a sense of belonging and stability.   Children who know a lot about their families tend to do better amidst chaos and tragedy. They tend to be more connected, attached, and resilient under stress. This was found to be the case after 911 and other situations. A good free resource for family history is: https://www.familysearch.org/

Some of the basic needs for everyone are described within Maslow's Hierarchy of Needs, such as: Food, Shelter, and Social Support. While these are not the only human needs, they are common for most.

For children, routines, traditions, and consistent relationships; being watched and cared for by the same loving adults is extremely important. Living with a revolving door of "significant other" relationships, and in many cases "barely significant other" relationships is incredibly unpredictable and stressful, even though it may seem to fill a void. Perhaps one of the most important questions for any parent in this situation might be: "am I motivated more by love or fear?" This question requires considerable honest introspection.

http://weight-lossnewsandresearch.blogspot.com/2017/09/maslow.html

Sometimes our best intentions can backfire. During World War II approximately two million children were evacuated from cities, from their families, often from their mother and perhaps grandparents, because their father had already left to fight in the war or may have been killed. These children went to foster homes in safer parts of Great Britain. While the move helped increase the physical safety of the children, the emotional results were mixed for both parents and children.

Sometimes, even in very chaotic situations where a child is moved and is likely to move again, there are things which may help. Help the child keep something of importance, such as a stuffed animal, blanket, or toy. Tell stories about grandparents and ancestors. Go someplace safe together and plant a tree that is likely to be taken care of and remain for the life of the child; for example (with permission), in a local park. These types of activities can help the child experience some stability, create lasting roots, and make connections, despite chaos and change.

3. Align expectations (of others AND self, appropriately and realistically.)

A common area of stress comes from inappropriate or unrealistic expectations of ourselves and others. We constantly see others who seem to have an easier and better life, better figure, more money, more power, better clothes, children who are better behaved, etc. Too often we see all that others have but don't see their struggles which almost invariably come sooner or later. We often compare ourselves against an unrealistic yardstick. As you work to improve some aspect of yourself, compare your new self to the person you were, not to someone else. Are you the same person you were twenty years ago? Have you made progress in some way, in any way?

> "Perhaps the best thing of all for me is to remember that my serenity is inversely proportional to my expectations. The higher my expectations of... and other people are, the lower is my serenity. I can watch my serenity level rise when I discard my expectations. But then "my rights" try to move in, and they too can force my serenity level down. I have to discard "my rights" as well as my expectations, by asking myself, "how important is it, really?" How important is it compared to my serenity, my emotional sobriety?" *Alcoholics Anonymous: The Big Book.*
>
> https://www.aa.org/pages/en_US/alcoholics-anonymous
>
> "Being in control of your life and having realistic expectations about your day-to-day challenges are the keys to stress management, which is perhaps the most important ingredient to living a happy, healthy and rewarding life." - Marilu Henner

Some of us tend to set unrealistic expectations for our children. While it is important to encourage and foster the best from our children, we can cause significant damage when the expectations are beyond their developmental ability. Sometimes very young children are required to care for even younger children. This can put the child-caregiver in a bind, set them up for failure, and create long-lasting rifts in what should be supportive relationships between siblings.

Another area of significant stress for far too many children is when they get the idea that your problems were caused by them. Sometimes this is blatant because some openly and directly blame the child. Sometimes one child can be specifically singled out for this ongoing blame. Even when not directly blamed, many children, far too often, get the idea that a separation or divorce is their fault. This is partly because young children begin life being egocentric. They believe everything revolves around them. Unfortunately, some people never lose this idea. Over time most children come to realize through healthy development that others have different opinions, different tastes, and the whole world doesn't revolve around them.

Hopefully children will come to learn and maintain the understanding that while they may not matter to everyone, they matter a great deal to some. If something lousy happens in your life, make sure the children around you understand it is not their fault. Never assume they understand until you have spoken and explained it to them

Consistent expectations for children is essential. When there are significantly different expectations between parents, or between one or two parents and others, such as the school, or perhaps a grandparent or other significant adults, this can be an underlying cause of frustration, confusion, manipulation, and even oppositional defiance. While not 100% true, there is partial truth in the adage: "when parents agree, children succeed."

It can be the same for some adults if the adult does not have a sound and grounded sense of who they are. Expectations can rise as abilities and maturity increase, they can decline with disability and failing health. However; even in these situations, there should be a degree of consistency if even on an upward or downward trajectory.

> A note of caution: I remember many years ago reading a piece of extremely wise advice from Dear Abby. In this column, she talked about the effect, criticizing a parent in front of a child can have on the child. At some level, children know they are also a part of that parent. If you say their mother or father is "no good," the child will often believe they are also "no good." If you feel you absolutely must criticize the parent of a child, never do it within earshot of the child. Children as well as adults communicate a great deal without speaking. In fact, most of our communication is unspoken. Be careful what you communicate even when not saying a word.

As discussed in this section, one of the fundamental sources of stress is inappropriate expectations for both self and others. When the expectations of others are completely unreasonable, a great deal of stress can build for both you and them. Adults have some responsibility for allowing these unreasonable expectations, placed upon them by others, to be stressful. Younger children on the other hand, will often not understand when an expectation for them is unreasonable. These unreasonable expectations can cause significant stress for children. Now there could be a great deal of disagreement on what a reasonable expectation may be. It is not the same for everyone. For example: you cannot expect someone to know what you are thinking (they may guess correctly from time to time, but it is an unreasonable expectation), and as mentioned previously, you cannot expect an 8 or 9-year-old child to cook all the meals or keep his or her baby sibling safe for extended periods of time. Neither, can you expect others to fix everything or take care of you all the time (unless you have a very significant disability, illness, and/or are very very young or very very old). Even the elderly and people with disabilities need to have reasonable responsibility and control over their own lives to the greatest extent possible. People feel better about themselves when they can do more for themselves. Self-determination, self-control, and self-sufficiency are ennobling and positively enabling. We all need to take responsibility for ourselves to the extent possible. For some of us, more is possible than we may wish to admit. Take responsibility and give credit!

Reasonable expectations and boundaries, can help create a feeling of safety, security and self-efficacy; when coupled with appropriate training, tools and support. Remember, what is reasonable is a moving target. Teach children new skills as they are ready. Provide support and opportunities. As you do this, expectations and usually trust can grow. Teach and allow children greater self-direction as they are ready. Do not share more information than is appropriate for developmental age or relationship.

> "The fault, dear Brutus, is not in our stars, but in ourselves." — William Shakespeare, Julius Caesar
>
> "Incredible change happens in your life when you decide to take control of what you do have power over instead of craving control over what you don't." — Steve Maraboli, Life, the Truth, and Being Free

Sometimes unhappiness comes not from what we do not have but from what we think we should have.

4. Increase resiliency.

What is resiliency? How do we increase resiliency?

There are many ways to increase resiliency, one is learning to deal with the small stuff. Don't sweat the small stuff. Don't tantrum, rage, or explode into a tirade. Take a deep breath, take a step back if needed, take a little break if needed, and remember the times when you've gotten through this in the past. Stop and remember there is a chance your interpretation of an event may not be complete or correct. You may only be seeing part of the picture. Learn to problem solve over little things. It will make it easier for you to problem solve over bigger and bigger things.

At least part of the beginning of the research on resilience came from research started in the 1950's in Hawaii. This research followed a group of individuals and families with significant life obstacles. Through the research, they found that about two thirds of the children of the group ended up with their own significant difficulties. Difficulties that might have been expected: dropping out of school, early pregnancy, drugs, alcohol, criminal activity, and various other problems such as described in the ACES study.

> http://weight-lossnewsandresearch.blogspot.com/2017/09/resilience-and-stress-research.html

> (Adverse Childhood Experiences (ACEs) https://www.cdc.gov/violenceprevention/acestudy/index.html)
>
> http://weight-lossnewsandresearch.blogspot.com/2017/10/aces-and-resilience.html

> Another resource for assessment and understanding adverse and

What caught the attention of the researchers, though, were the exceptions; children who grew up to overcome the numerous disadvantages they faced. These children developed resilience and though the researchers did not label it as such, self-efficacy.

> traumatic experiences is the ANSA.
>
> http://weight-lossnewsandresearch.blogspot.com/2018/01/ansa-and-adverse-experiences.html
>
> And the CANS for children and youth.
>
> http://weight-lossnewsandresearch.blogspot.com/2018/01/cans-and-adverse-childhood-experiences.html

From this early research came more research on resilience, much of this early research was conducted through university extension programs. Partially from the initial research on resilience, additional but similar veins of research were developed: Protective and Risk Factors, as well as Developmental Assets. Resilience and Developmental Assets are all primarily strength based approaches. A basic concept of strength based approaches is: **what you focus on increases**. This is not an invitation to hide your head in the sand and ignore problems which must be addressed. It is an invitation to find what is going well, what someone is doing right, then reinforcing, noticing, complimenting, and appreciating the positive. It is good to do the same for yourself.

This represented a huge paradigm shift as the social sciences have long looked at finding and attempting to fix problems. Strength based approaches look for

> "A man (or woman) should never be promoted to a managerial position if his (or her) vision focuses on people's weaknesses rather than on their strengths." Peter Drucker

strengths, assets, and resources and build upon what is already there and what can be added, extended, and expanded. Children and adults with greater resilience are better able to weather the storms of life with minimal stress.

Note: Research related to Developmental Assets found that, the more of these assets children had in their lives, the better they tended to do throughout their lives: emotionally, physically, and even financially.

Three primary *protective factors* which you can increase in yourself, and help others build are:

> Go to this webpage for links to research on developmental assets and stress: http://weight-lossnewsandresearch.blogspot.com/2017/08/developmental-assets-and-stress.html

1. Attachment

2. Initiation (self)

3. Self-control

> Go to the following webpage for links to research on

How to help yours or another child:

Attachment

> protective factors and stress reduction:
>
> http://weight-lossnewsandresearch.blogspot.com/2017/08/protective-factors-and-stress-reduction.html

Children, all of us really, need consistent supportive relationships. Help children develop deep friendships with peers who will support them and who they can support. Be a big, consistent, supportive part of your child's life... and the lives of other children. This does not mean you need to constantly hover, but you do need to know where they are, what they are doing, and who they are doing it with. Provide for and be involved in positive activities with yours and other children. It is important for children to develop good appropriate relationships with other adults who will mentor and support them, hopefully through much of their life. These relationships may be with relatives, band directors, scout leaders, 4 – H leaders, neighbors, coaches, church leaders, etc. Remember, it is your responsibility to assure that these adults will be good positive influences on your children. Unfortunately, there are some very dangerous, evil people out there; but, don't let that be an excuse for isolation. There are many good, supportive, loving, and caring people who want to help.

In many of these activities and programs you can and should participate with your child, sometimes while you are on the sidelines. For example: attend the 4-H meetings and T-Ball practice. Unless it is someone you know very well and absolutely trust, it is better to have activities in a public place and have more than one adult involved in any activity where you cannot attend yourself. Look for organizations that require background checks for leaders, though that is never a perfect guarantee.

Initiation

Give your child and other children appropriate opportunities (according to their developmental abilities) to initiate tasks, ideas, and problem solve on their own. When a child suggests... says, "let's" or "can we," or something similar, if it's appropriate, say "yes," or you may give a conditional yes. This might be something like: "after you do…" or you may need to give an alternative but similar suggestion and ask the child if the alternative is OK. One example of an alternative would be a child who sees a playground across a busy street and the child asks if the two of you can cross the street, right in the middle of the street. Your alternative suggestion might be that you walk to the corner where there is a crosswalk and stoplight, cross there and then go on to the playground. Another alternative may be that you visit a different playground soon. This doesn't mean you must or should do everything the child wants; though you should find opportunities to say "yes," at least some of the time. (Children, we all, need to learn boundaries, limits, and patience. When appropriate, it is also important for anyone to learn to cope with "no.") Be sure to be true to your word. Be trustworthy. If you tell your child that s/he can do something after doing ____ or that you can do something together after you finish ____ then make sure you follow through with your word after ____ is done.

Another way to teach this would be when a child comes to you with a problem. Instead of telling them how to solve the problem, ask what their ideas are. You may need to coax and shape the discussion a little to help them find an appropriate solution, or they may just come up with a great idea all on their own. When my oldest daughter was very young, she was plagued by nightmares with dark and scary ghosts. When we talked about this I asked her some questions and thinking of Casper the Friendly Ghost, I suggested that when she woke from such a dream she might replace the ghosts in her dream with one that looked and acted more like Casper. She immediately responded that, no, her ghost would be pink. It was the end of the nightmares. While I suggested a possible basic solution in this case, she came up with the final solution. Not just because of this, but she is someone who has no problems with self-initiation.

Self-control

Many years ago, some researchers brought a group of children together and one by one they were put in a room with a table and a marshmallow. They told each of the children they could eat the marshmallow now, or if they waited 15 minutes they could have two marshmallows. After the experiment, they followed these children for the next couple of decades. What they found was not surprising. The children who could wait for the gratification, those who had the better self-control, were significantly more successful in life. More recently a group of researchers with *VitalSmarts* conducted similar research on the same topic; however, they wanted to learn if the delayed gratification or self-control could be taught. They found that yes, it could be taught. Children and even adults can be taught skills of delayed gratification by teaching them techniques such as thinking about something other than the marshmallow. (Remember the concept of *Nature Abhors a Vacuum*.) You can teach a child or yourself to replace one thing with another more productive or healthy thought or action, or just an alternative thought or action that will work in the situation.

In my work with young children with developmental disabilities, and the service providers for these children, there is a basic concept I have tried to teach for about two decades. It is a concept which was expressed very well by the Star Trek character Spock, in The Wrath of Khan. In the movie, Spock declares, "*nature abhors a vacuum*." If you want a child or an adult, including yourself, to not do something, you must replace it with something TO DO. If you give a child, who needs to wait 15 minutes before eating a marshmallow, something to do while waiting, the child is much more likely to be able to wait. Self-control can be greatly aided by alternative activities.

You can learn greater self-control by using alternative and incompatible behaviors as will be discussed later in this book. You can also develop greater self-control by thinking about, in a quiet moment, times in your life when you were able to demonstrate better self-control. Write those down. Think about what was different or what you did differently. Recognize and duplicate your own success. When you are under a great deal of stress, it's difficult to do this; but, when you have a quiet moment, it may be easier. You may want to do this exercise with a trusted friend who can help remind you of your own past success. Celebrate and build on even your smallest successes.

For adults, the process is similar. Build resilience by:

1) Developing relationships with high levels of support and trust. Be the type of friend and support for others, you want others to be for you. Ask and learn what kind of support the other person needs and if appropriate, provide that type of support.

> Research on self-control and stress reduction:
> http://weight-lossnewsandresearch.blogspot.com/2017/08/self-control-and-stress-reduction.html
>
> Research on Developmental Assets was initially funded in part by The Lutheran Brotherhood. You can learn more here:
> http://www.learningtogive.org/resources/search-institute
>
> And here: http://www.search-institute.org/research/developmental-assets

2) Developing self-efficacy. Learn to do, understand, and develop, your positive capabilities or gifts in various aspects of life domains. According to your interests, develop physical skills to make or do good things.

3) Develop initiative. Learn as you go, understand that failure is feedback and feedback understood and applied correctly can lead to success. When you fail or fall (as we all do) get up and move forward.

4) Develop self-control. Learn techniques of stress management, self-calming, and develop appropriate flexibility. Develop good personal and interpersonal boundaries.

4b. Learned Helplessness, Depression, Despair, Fear, and Suicide

As I was putting the outline of this book together, I wanted to include some information on this topic; however, I wasn't sure if I wanted to put it under Resilience or Self-Efficacy. Both can have a profound impact on what I'll discuss here. As you can see, my decision was to place it in-between as its own sub-section.

A serious attempt at suicide is often a sign of absolute despair, a loss of or lack of hope. Unfortunately, suicide is a too frequent phenomenon in the United States and around the world. Initially I had included more information; however, I'll just leave you with one simple message. Any threat, discussion, or attempt of suicide, is an extremely serious matter and should be reported to an appropriate person or entity. Sometimes this is a local government mental health agency, some places it is a local hospital emergency room, or law enforcement. Report any concerns immediately and if you do not know where to turn, your local doctor, hospital, or law enforcement agency, should be able to direct you to the right place.

Depression is usually treatable. If you are experiencing feelings of depression, speak with your physician or a local mental health agency. Depression opens the door to addiction and moves the needle (influence) from Reflection towards Reaction. Depression makes it harder to think and make good rational choices. The default with depression is usually to react according to habit.

5. Increase self-efficacy.

> "If you don't think your anxiety, depression, sadness and stress impact your physical health, think again. All of these emotions trigger chemical reactions in your body, which can lead to inflammation and a weakened immune system. Learn how to cope, sweet friend." - Kris Carr

This statement may come as a surprise to many; but, one of the problems with today's society in the United States and many parts of the world has been the often over emphasis on self-esteem. Good self-esteem can be a great thing; however, self-esteem without appropriate boundaries, sense of responsibility, empathy and self-control can be dangerous. There are lots of criminals and politicians with great apparent self-esteem, to the point of narcissism. We all know, may be related to, and have probably worked with jerks who have great self-esteem... they think highly of themselves, or at least act like they do.

Often people without good self-efficacy and/or self-control tend to try to control others. This is frustrating and stressful for everyone. Help a child, yourself, or any individual build self-efficacy, help them develop appropriate boundaries, empathy, responsibility, and self-control and you will help them develop appropriate self-esteem.

> "We find that people's beliefs about their efficacy affects the sorts of choices they make in very significant ways. In particular, it affects their levels of motivation and

To develop self-efficacy, learn to do things; through observation, listening, reading, imitating, and taking small then increasingly larger steps until you are making the progress you are capable of. Take the time to listen, learn, and understand. Ask questions and seek deeper understanding about the things most important to you. So much information and superficial instant gratification is available at your fingertips today, few people take the time to learn deeply. Talking points and propaganda about this or that subject is all around us. Learn good critical thinking skills, the ability to listen patiently to multiple sides of an issue, and identify the truth amidst the rubbish.

> perseverance in the face of obstacles.
>
> Most success requires persistent efforts, so low self-efficacy becomes a self-limiting process. In order to succeed, people need a sense of self-efficacy, strung together with resilience to meet the inevitable obstacles and inequities of life." – Albert Bandura
>
> "Persons who have a strong sense of efficacy deploy their attention and effort to the demands of the situation and are spurred by obstacles to greater effort". – Albert Bandura
>
> "The content of most textbooks is perishable, but the tools of self-directness serve one well over time."– Albert Bandura

Learn to do good things, and then do them.

> "Well done is better than well said." - Benjamin Franklin

Self-Efficacy comes from:

Mastery Experience

Vicarious Experience: (Read about, watch others being successful. Watch or learn from others who overcame or have made the changes you want to make.)

Verbal Persuasion

Physiological States

Self-efficacy is context specific, an assessment of capabilities.

To increase self-efficacy, develop the habit of being a finisher. Get it done. Use lists; mark off what you have accomplished. I use a lot of electronic reminders, but LOVE Post-it notes for things to do. When the task is done, I throw the Post-it in the garbage... which gives me a great feeling of accomplishment! It is also a great stress release. If you have long lists, try tearing them up and throwing them away when everything is completed.

BE A FINISHER OF GOOD THINGS

BE A FINISHER OF GOOD DEEDS, WORK, SERVICE, PROJECTS, ACCEPTED ASSIGNMENTS

One of the most effective ways to teach someone what to do is to show him or her how to do it and then do it with them. The goal of modeling is to correctly demonstrate a target behavior to the person learning the new skill. Demonstrate, do the task or skill with them, then watch them complete the task or skill. Allow them to make insignificant mistakes. Provide loving targeted feedback. If they have made a mistake, tell them in a kind way, then help them make appropriate corrections. Children will learn a great deal (positive and/or negative) from observing the behavior of parents, siblings, peers, and teachers.

Without self-efficacy, we become terribly frustrated and obstructed by what should only be minimal speed bumps in life. The self-efficacious person will look for solutions, alternatives, or ways to move ahead, even without the typical tools or necessary understanding. They know they will figure it out along the way, find a way, and/or find someone who can help if necessary.

> I am better at this now than I was in the past, as my spouse and children will attest and likely co-workers, over the years. I love the concept portrayed by Shakespeare in: As You Like It: "Twas I, Tis Not I." This applies to every aspect of life. We do not need to continue to be who we have been.

Self-Efficacy can be taught. You can develop greater self-efficacy yourself. Learn from people who have done, accomplished, overcome, what you want to do. Volunteer to work with someone who can teach and mentor you. You are never too old to learn; but, you may be too proud to learn. To be humble is to be teachable. Start with the little things. Be faithful, dependable, and open to learning. If you do this and look for more opportunities to grow and have greater lessons and responsibilities, they will come.

> Distractions occur in our lives, at work, at home, everywhere, all the time. If we allow distractions to derail us, keep us from perusing our priorities, we will always chase distractions or just give up and give in. Learn to call these distractions, just that, "distractions." Learn to deal with them quickly or ignore them when they are trivial, get expert help if necessary--but focus on your priorities. Doing this will allow you to move forward and build self-efficacy. We can learn to be successful.

> "If you hear a voice within you say 'you cannot paint,' then by all means paint and that voice will be silenced."
> Vincent Van Gogh

http://weight-lossnewsandresearch.blogspot.com/2017/09/self-efficacy-and-stress-research.html

Don't just learn, learn to do stuff, learn to do good stuff, and learn to make stuff. Not just for you, but that which benefits others, especially those who might in some way be less fortunate. Providing anonymous or low profile and out of the spotlight service or gifts you have made is wonderful. You will help others and might even feel better about yourself.

It has been said: 'It is a lazy parent who does everything for their child'. It's usually easier to just do it all yourself; however, it's better to be patient, teach, and allow the child to mess up and learn. As the child learns, do the task with the child for a while if needed, then teach them to work independently. Don't sweat the small stuff!

"People who believe they have the power to exercise some measure of control over their lives are healthier, more effective and more successful than those who lack faith in their ability to effect changes in their lives." - Albert Bandura

"People who have a sense of self-efficacy bounce back from failure; they approach things in terms of how to handle them rather than worrying about what can go wrong." - Albert Bandura (You can learn to do this too.)

"Your best chance for being happy is to do the things that happy people do, live the way happy people live, and walk the path that happy people walk. As you do so, your chances to find joy in unexpected moments, to find peace in unexpected places, and to find the help of angels when you didn't even know they knew you existed improve exponentially." Jeffrey R. Holland

"The happiest people are those who do the most for others. The most miserable are those who do the least." - Booker T. Washington

For service opportunities check out: https://www.justserve.org/

6. Align values and behavior.

What does this mean?

How do we do this?

We bring a great deal of stress on ourselves when we do not do, what we deeply inside ourselves, believe is right. This is very close to the concept of *Cognitive Dissonance*. Almost all of us have values. Sometimes, though almost imperceptibly, values can show up in grandchildren and even great grandchildren that were not openly taught by the parents. I mention this because when our behaviors do not match our values, this causes an inner friction, sometimes called guilt, dissonance, uneasiness, or stress.

Clearly teach values to your children and coach them in living up to those values. Be a positive example of those values. Do not too easily discount the wisdom of the ages. Seek to understand your own values and align your behaviors with your values. Elevating behaviors, though it may be hard work at times, is almost always more healthy than rationalizing, or depressing values. We used to read and tell moral stories that helped build character and values. This doesn't happen as often as it once did. Books like *Aesop's Fables* and *The Book of Virtues* can be valuable resources in teaching children. Whoever; perhaps the most important book a child will read is the example of the adults they are with. Be an example of what you want them to be.

Don't just read to your children. Read and discuss. As they are able, have them read to you or take turns reading and discuss. Don't just tell them what you think; listen to what they think the message of the story is. Listen to their ideas first. You can add your thoughts; but don't discount theirs. Let them know their thoughts and ideas have value. Encourage them to express themselves. *The Adventures of Bobcat Family and Friends: Fastwater Takes a Swim* is an example of a story written for this kind of parent-child discussion. It is available on amazon.

> "What you are shouts so loudly in my ears I cannot hear what you say." - Ralph Waldo Emerson

Where you spend your time, and where you spend your money says a lot about your values. Does what you do, line up with what you say and/or think your values are? This was one of the catalysts that spurned me on to finally drop those 115+ pounds.

Reduce stress and guilt by improving behavior, not by lowering standards. It may seem difficult, especially in the midst of friends and associates that do otherwise. If you are not able to overcome negative social pressure, if you are not able to be the positive influence on your friends and associates, improve your social circle. This may sound harsh, but you cannot pull anyone out of the swamp (or manure) unless you are firmly standing on higher ground. Unfortunately, there are those who might prefer you remain in the swamp... with them.

> "If you desire truly to live you will cease trying to find magic tricks and short-cuts to life and learn the simple laws of being, and order your life in conformity with these. Realign your life with the laws of nature—this and this alone constitutes living to live." — Herbert M. Shelton, *Getting Well*
>
> "When wealth is lost, nothing is lost; when health is lost, something is lost; when character is lost, all is lost." - Billy Graham
>
> "When you were born, you cried and the world rejoiced.
>
> Live your life so that when you die, the world cries and you rejoice." White Elk

> Values, Behavior, and Stress Management:
>
> http://weight-lossnewsandresearch.blogspot.com/2017/08/values-

Is the way you live your life, your behavior and your choices, consistent with your fundamental values and beliefs. If it is not, there will be internal conflict and stress.

7. Improve physical health to the extent possible.

Establish *The Foundation* daily. Start with a, healthy, well balanced breakfast. Include protein, remember plant based is best. Include a small amount of fruit (avoid fruit juice). Include whole grains such as old fashioned rolled oats, barley, or brown rice. Include vegetables, especially vegetables with low starch. This may include leafy green or red vegetables, onions, peppers, carrots, zucchini, and/or tomatoes (which are a fruit but we won't get into that). (If you have diabetes, consult with your physician regarding what the best breakfast would look like for you.) Get in at least twenty minutes of aerobic exercise in the morning (build up to it if necessary). This could simply be a walk around the neighborhood with the dog, family member, and/or friend. Retire to your bed early and get a good night's sleep.

behavior-stress-reduction.html

"Moral justification is a powerful disengagement mechanism. Destructive conduct is made personally and socially acceptable by portraying it in the service of moral ends. This is why most appeals against violent means usually fall on deaf ears." - Albert Bandura

Note: Do not confuse guilt with shame. Guilt, if harnessed and responded to effectively, can help propel us to self-improvement and positive change. Shame, on the other hand, often leads to depression and hopelessness. Hopelessness rarely leads to positive change.

"You may fill your heads with knowledge or skillfully train your hands, but unless it is based upon high, upright character, upon a true heart, it will amount to nothing. You will be no better than the most ignorant." - Booker T. Washington

"You can't hold a man down without staying down with him." - Booker T. Washington

A substantial, healthy, well-balanced breakfast, helps reduce cravings throughout the day. Food Security helps reduce cravings.

Go to this webpage for research on physical health, condition, and stress management:

http://weight-lossnewsandresearch.blogspot.com/2017/08/physical-health-condition-and-stress.html

8. Have fun and enjoy good humor.

There are basically two different types of humor in the world. There is the kind that divides and puts people down and the type that unites. One increases stress, the other decreases stress.

What's the difference?

When I was young, Polish jokes were popular. When I lived in Eastern Canada, jokes about people from Newfoundland were popular. As a college student, I remember a friend from Norway tell me a joke about Swedes. I still remember the joke. I still don't "get it" but I remember it. Today it is still common to tell jokes about someone who may be different from you. Sometimes putting others down is an effort to feel better about yourself, but it never works well for long and long-term it always causes more stress and dissonance than it relieves. Remember, there are people in the world who gain power from creating division hatred, and fear.

When we make jokes about or put down a parent or grandparent of a child in front of that child, at some level the child will take it personally. They almost always, intuitively understand they are a part of that person and if there is something wrong with that person there is something wrong with them. Please, never put down your ex, or a child's grandparents in front of the child. Do not make jokes about others for any reason. Ultimately, it is unhelpful and demeans you as well as them. Learn to use and share healthy humor.

> "There are two ways of exerting one's strength: one is pushing down, the other is pulling up." - Booker T. Washington (This includes inner strength)

> "The ability to laugh -- either naturally or as learned behavior -- may have important implications in societies such as the U.S. where heart disease remains the number one killer," .... "We know that exercising, not smoking, and eating foods low in saturated fat will reduce the risk of heart disease. Perhaps regular, hearty laughter should be added to the list."
>
> ... It may be possible to incorporate laughter into our daily activities, just as we do with other heart-healthy activities, such as taking the stairs instead of the elevator. "We could perhaps read something humorous or watch a funny video and try to find ways to take ourselves less seriously,".... Laughter Is Good For Your Heart, According To A New University Of Maryland Medical Center Study: November 2000; Michael Miller, M.D., F.A.C.C., director of the Center for Preventive Cardiology at the University of Maryland Medical Center
>
> https://www.sciencedaily.com/releases/2000/11/001116080726.htm

> "The recommendation for a healthy heart may one day

Humor changes your physiology and reduces stress.

Many years ago, I taught a workshop for single adults with disabilities, and single parents. During the workshop, we would touch on the importance of humor. At that time, I would show a short video with *Humphrey the Bear*. You can find some of these on YouTube.

9. Improve (or change) your physiological state.

One of the best ways to do this is with mindfulness meditation combined with aerobic exercise, such as walking. (We'll talk more about mindfulness meditation later.)

Another way to change your physiology is through deep breathing. Deep breathing while stretching can be helpful because it can change your physiology.

ACTIVITY:

Learn to blow BIG bubbles.

Take some bubble soap and a wand and practice blowing bubbles. Blow bubbles as large as you can. You must blow slow and steady. Take deep breaths to blow BIG bubbles. This is an easy way to help older children, teens, and even adults, learn and relearn to breathe slowly and deeply. Doing this, changes your physiology and helps reduce stress.

Practice using your stomach to take BIG breaths. (Most of us get into the habit of only taking shallow chest breaths.) Breathe in through your nose and out through your mouth.

Put your hand on your stomach and feel if your stomach is moving up and down as you breathe... taking big, deep, belly breaths

Combine deep breathing and stretching.

Face scrunches: For this exercise, breathe in through your nose, then hold your breath while scrunching up your face tightly, closing your eyes, and holding for a couple of seconds. Breath out slowly while relaxing your muscles and opening your eyes. Repeat a couple, three, or four

---

be exercise, eat right and laugh a few times a day." -- Michelle Murray

For more research on fun and humor for stress reduction, go to this webpage:

http://weight-lossnewsandresearch.blogspot.com/2017/08/fun-humor-in-stress-reduction.html

"Laughter is important, not only because it makes us happy, it also has actual health benefits. And that's because laughter completely engages the body and releases the mind. It connects us to others, and that in itself has a healing effect." - Marlo Thomas

"Hearty laughter is a good way to jog internally without having to go outdoors." - Norman Cousins

times. Don't do this while doing any activity where you need your eyes, such as driving. Please keep your eyes open while driving.

Half neck turns: Start with your head down, breathe in through your nose. As you are breathing in, slowly turn your head to the right and back (without causing yourself any pain). Hold... then breathe out while you relax and bring your head down in front of you. Repeat to the left.

Shoulder Shrugs: Start with your head down. Breathe in through your nose and slowly raise your shoulders and head as high as you can without causing any pain. Hold the position and your breath, then slowly relax your shoulders and allowing your head to drop forward while breathing out. Repeat multiple times.

Body Droop: Stand against a wall with your body bent forward and your arms down in a relaxed position. Breathe in through your nose slowly and raise your body and arms until you are standing straight up with your arms up and stretch. Hold, and then slowly breathe out through your mouth while relaxing your body. Repeat.

There are a whole series of breathing exercises combined with muscle tightening and relaxing which can be found in: _Minding The Body, Mending the Mind_ by Joan Borysenko.

> Go to the following webpage for research on deep breathing, yoga, stretching, tai chi, and stress management: http://weight-lossnewsandresearch.blogspot.com/2017/08/deep-breathing-yoga-tai-chi-and-stress.html

10. Develop and Maintain Healthy Supportive Relationships.

Does anyone know what that is anymore???

Two stories:

a. Roseto, Pennsylvania Study

Many years ago, there was a community in Pennsylvania, where the residents were much healthier than the nation, on average. Scientists decided to study this community, thinking they would have all these great health habits. What they found was; the relationships, connections, and support in the community, produced a profound benefit for the physical health of the residents.

> "People who seek psychotherapy for psychological, behavioral or relationship problems tend to experience a wide range of bodily complaints...The body can express emotional issues a person may have difficulty processing consciously...I believe that the vast majority of people don't recognize what their bodies are really telling them. The way I see it, our emotions are music and our bodies are instruments that play the discordant tunes. But if we don't know how to read music, we just think the instrument is defective." — Charlette Mikulka

> "The power of community to create health is far greater than any physician, clinic or hospital." - Mark

b. Children's Hospital and the old German Cleaning Woman

Hyman

Another great story is one about a children's hospital many years ago. At that time, a large percentage of babies who needed extensive hospitalization, died. One wing of one hospital started having better success with more babies living and being able to eventually leave the hospital and return to their family. What they found was the night cleaning lady, instead of doing her job cleaning, was holding babies. (One of the morals of this story is that while sanitation is important, good touch, holding, and social support, are essential for most if not all of us.)

Being a good problem solver is very important for stress reduction and management. We have also talked about developing skills such as self-efficacy; however, **"Never let a problem to be solved become more important than a person to be loved." Thomas S. Monson**

~

Always remember that: sometimes saying "I'm sorry" means you care more about a relationship than being right.

Be humble enough to apologize to your spouse, children, and others when needed. We ALL have need to apologize from time to time. Try to see and understand another's point of view.

For information on supportive relationships and stress, go to this webpage: http://weight-lossnewsandresearch.blogspot.com/2017/08/relationships-support-and-stress.html

The following is from Four Things Successful People Do To Have Great Relationships by Marshall Goldsmith and Alan Weiss.

1. "We have to give to get. For relationships to be fulfilling we have to invest in them; we can't simply be takers. What we offer needn't be tangible (although it can be); it can be listening, support, feedback, or empathy. Relationships are two-way streets. You can't hog the road.

2. Relationships are based on trust. Trust is the belief that the other person has your best interests in mind and that you have his/her best interests in mind. Honest feedback and advice, even when painful, are part of caring for the other person.

3. Relationships are not a zero-sum game. For me to win, you don't have to lose. For you to win, I don't have to lose. We can both win (or lose). I am not diminished by your victories. We rejoice in success and bemoan loss for either party.

For youth especially, whose brains are still so very malleable and immature, and who do not have the engrained habitual skills to make consistent healthy choices, a smart phone, tablet, or even computer access in isolation can become an open window to a plethora, a "Pandora's Box," of potential addictions. These include addictions in: video gaming, violence, social isolation, gambling, pornography, shopping, and other anti-social behaviors. While not all will become addicted, almost all who have unfettered access will be exposed and most will be affected in one way or another. There are better and less expensive options for electronic communication such as flip phones (yes, sounds very "old school"). There are also safer options for computer and internet access such as a computer in a well-traveled, non-secluded area of the home. (The perfect software for parental controls, to my knowledge, does not exist.) Too many youth and young adults are not learning healthy communication through face to face interactions. So much of communication is nonverbal or non-written. Without good face to face communication skills, it is difficult to develop and maintain healthy relationships. Spend time face to face with your friends, and your children, without electronics. It may be anxiety provoking at first if you do not have good personal communication skills, but over time, healthy and supportive relationships will reduce overall stress for everyone involved.

> 4. Relationships need to be appropriate. If you're promoted, your former colleagues are now subordinates, and your former superiors are now peers. You can reach a level of familiarity and ease in a personal relationship that may not be right for a professional relationship. Similarly, social relationships have their own unspoken rules. You probably wouldn't act the same way with your college friends as you would with your prospective mother-in-law."
>
> http://www.marshallgoldsmith.com/articles/4-things-successful-people-do-to-have-great-relationships/

Any addiction can and is likely to distort positive, supportive relationships which are essential for good health, both physical and emotional. Any addiction will hinder the addict from developing the deep emotionally supportive relationships which may otherwise be possible. While everyone who is wise will stay as far away from the edge (see chapter on avoiding) as possible, and anyone who does not, can become addicted, teen/adolescent brains are especially susceptible to developing addictions.

Recently the World Health Organization declared Internet Addiction, as an addiction, which it was before it was declared as such.

> http://weight-lossnewsandresearch.blogspot.com/2017/09/addiction-and-adolescent-brain.html
>
> http://weight-lossnewsandresearch.blogspot.com/2018/01/internet-addiction.html
>
> http://weight-lossnewsandresearch.blogspot.com/2018/01/smartphone-and-teen-suicide.html

> "We were keeping our eye on 1984. When the year came

Many websites do whatever they can, to addict you, hold you on the site and bring you back as often as possible. Their purpose is to make money with your presence, and/or influence your thinking and behavior. Some people are so addicted to these enticements they give others their passwords and enlist them to access their account in the *'dreadful'* situations when they cannot access the internet themselves. This behavior is not healthy and does not lead to healthy relationships. Healthy, deeply intimate, health building and sustaining relationships simply cannot be developed online. Many today, especially youth and young adults, have never experienced, and lack the skills to develop deep quality relationships; confusing the counterfeit with the genuine. If this is an area where you struggle, all is not lost. Unplug for periods of time, turn it off and put it down. Play board games. Visit the elderly and others in nursing homes. Volunteer. Learn to listen with patience. It may sound dreadful at first, but you may also come to enjoy personal interactions with even dissimilar people more than you could have ever imagined. Many things we have been programmed and have come to believe to be essential were luxuries or not even dreamed of by our ancestors and barely a *"pipe dream"* by many of the less fortunate today. Much of what we allow to envelope us is trivial and superficial to include much of the information or misinformation we hear or read.

> and the prophecy didn't, thoughtful Americans sang softly in praise of themselves. The roots of liberal democracy had held. Wherever else the terror had happened, we, at least, had not been visited by Orwellian nightmares.
>
> But we had forgotten that alongside Orwell's dark vision, there was another - slightly older, slightly less well known, equally chilling: Aldous Huxley's Brave New World. Contrary to common belief even among the educated, Huxley and Orwell did not prophesy the same thing. Orwell warns that we will be overcome by an externally imposed oppression. But in Huxley's vision, no Big Brother is required to deprive people of their autonomy, maturity and history. As he saw it, people will come to love their oppression, to adore the technologies that undo their capacities to think.
>
> What Orwell feared were those who would ban books. What Huxley feared was that there would be no reason to ban a book, for there would be no one who wanted to read one. Orwell feared those who would deprive us of information. Huxley feared those who would give us so much that we would be reduced to passivity and egoism. Orwell feared that the truth would be concealed from us. Huxley feared the truth would be drowned in a sea of irrelevance. Orwell feared we would become a captive culture. Huxley feared we would become a trivial culture, preoccupied with some equivalent of the feelies, the orgy porgy, and the centrifugal bumblepuppy. As Huxley remarked in Brave New World Revisited, the civil libertarians and rationalists who are ever on the alert to oppose tyranny "failed to take into account man's almost infinite appetite for distractions." In 1984, Orwell added, people are controlled by inflicting pain. In Brave New World, they are controlled by inflicting pleasure. In short, Orwell feared that what we fear will ruin us. Huxley feared that what we desire will ruin us.
>
> This book is about the possibility that Huxley, not Orwell, was right." — Neil Postman, <u>Amusing Ourselves to Death</u>

No matter how healthy your choices or behavior, if you live long enough, your health is likely to wane; but love, if it's genuine, will not. Do the hard work to develop deep personal, supportive relationships. If you don't know how, volunteer to work with those who do. This is not advice to give up technology. I'm writing this using technology; but do not allow technology to control or consume your life. If you are already addicted and cannot let it go, you may have to completely sever your chains with technology, for at least a time. Here's a test. Go for a week without the internet, computers, televisions, or anything high tech. If the test creates significant anxiety or depression, you may be addicted and you may need help.

Take a walk with someone; perhaps in a forest, along a green belt, or just in the neighborhood. Practice listening and sharing. There are so many who have a great need to be listened to, and experience empathy. Walking and talking has many health benefits. Many are more comfortable sharing and talking side by side, than face to face. Walking and physically working together, can be a great way to get to know your kids, or anyone. Walking together without pressing for conversation allows tension to dissipate, often resulting in more meaningful conversations. Debate less. Love and listen more. Ask people to tell you more. Listen with genuine interest.

> "Treasure the love you receive above all. It will survive long after your good health has vanished." - Og Mandino

Recently a man in one of the addiction recovery groups my wife and I facilitate, made an especially insightful comment. He said that while he had not cheated on his wife sexually, he realized he had not been faithful to her or their son because he had allowed himself to be consumed by his addiction instead of giving the time and energy, to his wife and family, they needed and deserved.

> "He who would do great things should not attempt them all alone." – Seneca

Belong to organizations. If you have a spouse or significant other, participate together. (Yes, some alone time is important, but not to the detriment of relationships.) Get to know your neighbors.

> "But you were always a good man of business, Jacob," faltered Scrooge, who now began to apply this to himself. ... "Mankind was my business. The common welfare was my business; charity, mercy, forbearance, and benevolence, were, all, my business." responded the ghost of Jacob Marley in A Christmas Carol by Charles Dickens.

When I was in my first year of college, I didn't have many friends, and was not at all popular. I Never was, I have never been "cool," but that's OK. I decided to look around for other people who didn't seem to have many friends, and befriend them. It made a huge difference in my life and the lives of others. There are ample people out there, longing for a friend. You don't have to have a bunch. You don't have to be a "social butterfly." Develop a few good supportive relationships.

11. Mindfulness Meditation.

Mindfulness meditation is a form of meditation in which people learn to pay attention to what they are doing at the moment for a sustained period of time.

Insight is similar to mindfulness meditation. This type of meditation helps one concentrate on the present. This technique allows you to let go of the past and future thoughts. During mindfulness meditation, you focus on the moment.

For Mindfulness Meditation:

a. Enjoy the activity (like it was new every time)

b. Lose track of time

c. Be totally in the moment

Mindfulness Meditation is absolutely individual. What is relaxing for one may not be for another. This can be accomplished alone or with another person. While it may be possible, it can become more difficult in larger groups.

Here are some possibilities to consider.

Bathing (soaking in a hot or warm tub)

Cleaning

Dishes (hand washing)

Driving (car, motorcycle, ATV, etc.)

Games (especially table games where there isn't any tension or need for competition)

Gardening

Hiking

Home Repairs

Laundry

Music (the right kind of course which we discuss in another section)

Painting (either artistic or painting a house or fence)

Pets (spending time with, petting, walking with, etc.)

Playing

Reading

Running

Video Games: I mention video games because they can be very effective for some and they can be totally absorbing. However; I hesitated to add this because they can also become very addictive and harmful in the long term. I have used video games for this in the past and it has been effective. Unfortunately, it came to a point when I was young, where I almost lost a job due to having become addicted to a video game. I do not play them at all anymore and do not encourage others to play video games. For some it can be extremely effective. If you can do it for no more than a couple hours no more than one time per week, it may be OK. Anything more than that and you are flirting with a dangerous addiction, and a colossal waste of time. If it's not something you do, don't start. If you do it for more than a couple hours a week, stop and find something better. Any addiction adds stress to your life and diminishes relationships.

Currently (2018) it is estimated in the United States that 20% of young men between the ages of 18 and 28 are addicted to online gaming. It is perhaps the fastest growing addiction in the world and had become epidemic in China.

Here are more healthy options for mindfulness meditation:

Showering

Talking: Either just chatting or having a deep conversation with someone.

Walking

Writing or Journaling: There are multiple benefits from this. If what you write is personal and you don't want it shared, keep it safe and secure.

Do something where you feel like you've accomplished something when you are done, something that does not take a long time, perhaps a one or two-hour craft or project. This may provide the added benefit of feeling you have finished something and you will have increased self-efficacy.

The key to know if the meditation has been effective or not, is how you feel when you are done. If you are more relaxed and

> Video gaming and excessive internet use can be extremely detrimental to child and adolescent brain development.
> http://weight-lossnewsandresearch.blogspot.com/2017/10/video-games-internet-and-developing.html
>
> Also: http://weight-lossnewsandresearch.blogspot.com/2017/11/depression-and-video-games.html
>
> http://weight-lossnewsandresearch.blogspot.com/2017/11/depression-and-internet.html
>
> http://weight-lossnewsandresearch.blogspot.com/2017/11/screen-time-and-depression.html

> http://weight-lossnewsandresearch.blogspot.com/2017/09/mindfulness-and-stress-research.html

refreshed when you are done, even if you are a *bit* sore from physical exertion, consider it time well spent.

12. Develop an Attitude of Gratitude: learn to say please and thank you and mean it.

> "Be thankful for a breath of fresh air to be alive and well. Allow love and happiness to penetrate throughout your mind and soul. Take time to relax and live in the moment, the now, the present. Enjoy today." – Amaka Imani Nkosazana

Learn and practice The Happiness Secret.

Abraham Lincoln experienced many family deaths, including three children. He suffered with lifelong chronic depression and had numerous setbacks. Still, he found reasons to be grateful, positive, and empathetic. Perhaps some of his empathy grew out of his trials and tribulations, of which he had many.

> Go to the following webpage if you would like to read research on the subject:
>
> http://weight-lossnewsandresearch.blogspot.com/2017/08/stress-management-and-gratitude.html

When we first started facilitating an addiction recovery group for a group of men who are incarcerated, many of them had been transferred from another location. I remember one or more of them commenting on how grateful they were to have been relocated to a place where they could see mountains and deer. I also remember many commenting on being grateful for having been caught and having the opportunity to change their lives.

> "Most folks are about as happy as they make up their minds to be." – Abraham Lincoln

13 Listen to and Enjoy Relaxing Music

> This reminds me of a poem I've heard and which has been attributed to more than one individual. "Two men look out the self-same bars. One sees the mud. The other the stars."

The music you listen to for this purpose must be enjoyable to you, but also genuinely relaxing.

Many years ago, as a children's therapist, I was talking with a young man about relaxing music. He said he relaxed to Metallica. I did not confront him, but suggested we "check it out". I asked him to bring some Metallica in the next week when we got together. I hooked him up to some simple bio-feedback equipment and explained to him what would happen as he relaxed or became tenser. I then turned on the music and left the room. When the song had finished, I returned to the room and we looked at the readings together. He concluded that Metallica was not as relaxing as he thought.

Very relaxing music will be more like baroque and less like Metallica; however, some people hate baroque music and so this would not be a good type of music for relaxation for everyone. For some people, old country music may be very relaxing. The rhythm of relaxing music will be slower to match slower breathing, a slower heartbeat, and more relaxed brainwaves. You will be able to enjoy the music at a lower volume. Baroque is great for some because it often does all of these. Pachelbel's Canon can be particularly good because it matches an almost perfect brainwave for learning and relaxation.

One of the keys to relaxing music, as well as other stress reduction and relaxation exercises is the understanding that almost no one can go from 75 miles per hour to 25 miles per hour in just a couple seconds and feel relaxed. Have you ever been driving on a freeway at 75 mph and turned into a town where you had to immediately slow down to 25 mph? For many this can cause a bit of anxiety for at least a short period of time. Something internally wants to speed up and this can cause anxiety. It is the same with music. If you are really stressed or anxious and sit or lay down and start listening to something like Pachelbel's Cannon, even if you like that type of music, it can cause more stress than it relieves, at least for a while. Some people can be going 'a million miles an hour, then immediately lie down and go to sleep. Many of us do best with a routine and time to wind down before falling asleep. This is also one of the reasons it can be difficult to wrestle with the kids one minute and then put them to bed the next. Bedtime routines that help prepare and relax, can be extremely helpful for most children <u>and</u> adults. When using music to help you relax, if your mind and body have been going 75 or 80 miles per hour, you may want to start with a beat in-between where you are at, and the slow even rhythm of Pachelbel's Cannon or something similarly slow and relaxing. (Pachelbel's Cannon, or something similar may be too slow and actually irritating.) You may want to start with some easy listening music. Personally, I like old Rhythm and Blues (I especially love The Drifters and Sam Cooke), Country, Michael Buble', or Andrea Bocelli.

No matter the techniques you are using for relaxation, transitioning from 75 to 25 or even slower (sleep) can take longer for some than others. Routines (done the same repeatedly) that gradually help you or others step down and relax can be very helpful. Routines provide cues that tell your mind, help your mind and body relax. Cues such as smells, routines, and music, can help change us from stressed to relaxed and can become habitual as we repeat and practice.

Remember, when you use music, it must be both relaxing and enjoyable for you… or the child if you are trying to help a child relax.

ACTIVITY:

Stop and listen to a slow, quiet, relaxing piece of music. This could be some kinds of country music, something New Age, or Pachelbel's Cannon.

The version of Pachelbel's Cannon I often like to use IF I am prepared for deeper relaxation is by Daniel Kobialka. Find music that works well for you and listen to it when you need to and are prepared to relax.

14. Create a relaxing place: (create context, cues, routines, and other conditioning for relaxation).

> Go to the following webpage for links to research on baroque music and stress reduction:
>
> http://weight-lossnewsandresearch.blogspot.com/2017/08/baroque-music-and-stress-reduction.html

Create a place where you go which is only for relaxing. Avoid thinking of anything stressful in that place, listen to and enjoy relaxing music, never watch TV there, never argue there. Make it your place to relax and rejuvenate. This may be in your home, but does not have to be. (When I was young, there were two places I would go with my horse.)

There may be a park close to where you live, or a room in the library. It could be where you go to read an enjoyable book. It could be a break room at work. Even if there are other people there, it **can be** your quiet and relaxing place. When needed and stressed, if you cannot go there, you can imagine yourself there, safe and relaxed. There is a beautiful quiet beach in the Olympic National Park I have often thought of for relaxation.

15. Live within your means, spend less than you make.

> "My stove is old. My wallpaper is old. It's the same wallpaper from when I moved here and I never changed it. Why would I change it? I just keep it clean. If you take better care of things, you can hold onto them longer. That's how I still run things. If it works, I keep it. If it doesn't, I see if I can use it for something else. If I can't, and I usually can, I toss it." ― Clara Cannucciari, Clara's Kitchen: Wisdom, Memories, and Recipes from the Great Depression
>
> "We really never, never threw anything away. You think you know about recycling? We invented it. We had to. We were desperate. Sometimes maybe the only thing we had to work with was a couple of leftover baked potatoes from the weekend, and that was all there was to eat. Didn't matter to us that much. Ma just baked them again. Twice-Baked Potatoes really were kind of a treat for us, and we'd never complain when she served them." ― Clara Cannucciari, Clara's Kitchen: Wisdom, Memories, and Recipes from the Great Depression
>
> "Being frugal does not mean being cheap! It means being

Teach children to do the same.

16. Simplify

Whenever

Wherever possible

Set priorities. You cannot do everything. There may be hundreds or thousands of demands on your time and attention. If you try to address all of them, if you try to do everything, you won't do anything well. This includes all the things mentioned in this book. Start with just one or two of the easiest changes you might be able to make. Once you have them down, add another, etc.

In this book, I go into some depth on goal setting. One of the crucial aspects of setting and writing your goals is to prioritize. You, like me, have only 24 hours in a day. People who focus on one or a few achievable goals at a time are much more likely to achieve those goals than people who try to do too much or those who give up and don't try at all.

Do not allow yourself to be distracted by the many superficial speed bumps of life.

Unplug from technology… and let it go, at least periodically for a time. Most programs on television, most movies, and much if not most, of the internet is a colossal waste of time keeping you from what matters most and what will bring you and others greater happiness, health, and even wealth. When at all possible, face to face is much more valuable than "face-time", though for distant friends and relatives, there is certainly value to "face-time".

---

economical and avoiding waste."- Catherine Pulsifer

"Annual income twenty pounds, annual expenditure nineteen six, result happiness. Annual income twenty pounds, annual expenditure twenty pound ought and six, result misery." –Charles Dickens

"Many people take no care of their money till they come nearly to the end of it, and others do just the same with their time." –Johann Wolfgang von Goethe

Stop and think a minute about this last one, make sure you do not do the same. As I've often heard others say, 'none of us will get out of this life alive.' Don't wait until the end of your time to make your time more meaningful and enjoyable. Don't wait to make a positive difference in the lives of others.

"People don't realize how easy they have it these days. Most kids have never known what it's like to go without anything. They want something, they get it. If there isn't enough money, they charge it. We never wanted anything because we never realized we could have anything. We never missed what we never had. Things were much simpler back then, and we were stronger for it. We worked together to keep the house in order, to put food on the table. We kept things going." — Clara Cannucciari, Clara's Kitchen: Wisdom, Memories, and Recipes from the Great Depression

"I have on my office wall a wise and useful reminder by Anne Morrow Lindbergh concerning one of the realities of life. She wrote, 'My life cannot implement in action the demands of all the people to whom my heart responds.' That's good counsel for us all, not as an excuse to forego duty, but as a sage point about pace and the need for quality in relationships" - Neal A Maxwell

17. Let Go and Forgive

There is so much of importance here they could easily be divided into many sub-sections. However; because there is so much that overlaps, I am keeping it all together and hope it is presented in a way which is helpful and meaningful. Sometimes letting go is forgiving. Sometimes letting go includes making amends, apologizing and asking forgiveness for having done something wrong or hurting someone else. Sometimes letting go actually requires taking responsibility. It is difficult to change anything about yourself without acknowledging the needed change, and your own responsibility. Remember: **Take Responsibility Give Credit**. It's hard to let go of a fault, you don't know you have. Sometimes this process requires the help of a trusted friend, counselor, or advisor.

After having done everything you can or need to do to take responsibility and/or make amends, sometimes you need to forgive yourself and just let go. Yes, I know, sometimes this is easier said than done. Self-sabotage in any addiction recovery or just general weight loss is a common problem. Some of us have lingering thoughts that we don't really deserve to be healthy, be loved, and sometimes that we don't even deserve to live (if this is a serious problem for you, seek professional help). Let go of those feelings. Be open to love, to forgiveness. Learn to love yourself. As you follow the steps outlined and the programs mentioned in this book, you can come to believe you deserve to be loved and successful. As any of us heal, we are in a better position to help lift others. Help others, provide empathy, compassion, and lift others where you can, you will reap more benefits than the efforts you extend.

Whenever you let go of one thing, replace it with something better.

Sometimes you need to forgive others (that does not mean they do not need to face the consequences for things they may have done to you or others). You can forgive someone, letting go of the emotional weight of hatred or resentment, and still take measures to keep yourself and others safe.

> "All too often women believe it is a sign of commitment, an expression of love, to endure unkindness or cruelty, to forgive and forget. In actuality, when we love rightly we know that the healthy, loving response to cruelty and abuse is putting ourselves out of harm's way." — Bell Hooks, All About Love: New Visions

In the 12 step videos, we share, and from many of the men in one of the groups we lead, I have heard many say it was a relief, and they were grateful they were caught. Getting caught was the catalyst, perhaps because they had hit rock bottom, for them to begin to heal. I know this is not so for many, but for some it is an opportunity to change their life and in some cases, begin to repair the damage they have done to themselves and others.

Many years ago, I co-taught a class that included the concept of letting-go. My co-teacher would be in the class speaking with the group and I would walk in late with an obvious heavy backpack and start complaining about the pain and weight. When people would suggest I remove the pack I would continue to complain and look very uncomfortable but ignore their comments. Finally, I would take the backpack off, still holding it, but would begin to take very large rocks out of the pack. One by one I would explain what each rock represented, some past hurt or offence, and place it on the table with a thud.

The point was how much it hurts **us** when we carry hatred and resentment around. I remember one time one of the rocks disappeared. I found out later that one of the women in the class had carefully wrapped a rock up in tissue and placed it in her purse. It took her a while to be able to let it go.

Heavy rocks are a terrible burden for you to carry around the rest of your life. Let go of hatred (including self-hatred), resentment, and grudges.

There is an old story of two monks who had taken a vow of silence and were never to speak with or touch women. The two monks were walking along a trail and came across a fast stream with the bridge out. There was a woman looking very worried at the rushing waters. One of the monks picked her up without saying a word and carried her across, placing her safely on the other side. The two continued on their journey for the rest of the day. At sunset, when they could speak, the monk who had not picked up the women angrily asked the other how he could have picked up and carried the woman earlier that morning. The other, wiser monk responded: "Dear brother, I put her down this morning, it is you who have carried her all day."

> "I shall allow no man to belittle my soul by making me hate him." - Booker T. Washington
>
> "He who takes offense when offense was not intended is a fool, yet he who takes offense when offense is intended is an even greater fool for he has succumbed to the will of his adversary." — Brigham Young

Perhaps I really work hard at trying to forgive quickly because I am keenly aware of so much for which I have need to be forgiven.

Here are some techniques that may help you let go.

If you are angry with someone, you may tell them, but in a kind and non-confrontational way. <u>Crucial Conversations</u> from VitalSmarts may help you learn how to do this more effectively.

Helps in letting go:

Write it out, cut it up, burn it in a safe place, throw it away, bury it and plant something new over it. Tie it to a balloon and let it go (be careful as someone may read it)

Step away, take a walk, and try deep breathing and stretching.

Let go of rumination. Replace those thoughts with something more pleasant such as a song, poem, or something you are looking forward to doing. For children, you may want to distract with another thought or activity. However; when there is something of significance that is bothering a child, they usually need a way to appropriately process those thoughts or memories. For anyone, children or adults, it can be dangerous to bury something that needs to be told to an appropriate adult. Sometimes a professional counselor can help children disclose things that need to be told through play or art. Drawing a picture of an event or feeling can sometimes be helpful, especially if discussed in a loving, supportive, and caring manner. Sometimes the discussion can take place as a metaphor, and for now that may be enough. Drawing a picture, making a collage, and then destroying or burying it can be effective for an adult or child.

There is a wonderful book which I have read many times: <u>Love is Letting Go of Fear</u>. It is short, easy to read, and profound. I would recommend it for anyone.

Sometimes we need to reexamine our interpretation of events or what someone may have said. Consider how you might rewrite the story in your mind to lessen or eliminate what you may perceive to be an offense. Your perception, even if a partial truth may not be, probably is not, the whole truth.

Sometimes we need to let go of stubborn and sometimes prideful positions.

Hugh Prather once asked: **'would you rather be happy or would you rather be right?'** Sometimes that is a real choice.

Be the type of person who is slow to be offended. You may know what someone did, but you may never completely know why they did it. The truth is; they may not entirely know why they did it... whatever IT is. While we

> "You measure the size of the man (or woman) by the size of the things that makes him (or her) mad." Attributed (with slight variations) to both Benjamin Franklin and Adlai Stevenson
>
> "Life is 10% what happens to you and 90% how you react to it". Charles R. Swindoll

have a responsibility to do our best to be kind, we also have a responsibility to do our best to **not** be offended.

Letting go of things outside your control does not mean you must be totally silent. There are many times in my work and other situations where I disagree with something and I let people know in a professional and polite way that I disagree. I state my opinion, and then let it go because it is out of my control and/or outside of my authority.

Sometimes you may be in a situation where you have significant disagreement for ethical or moral reasons and in those cases, you may need to express your opinion in a professional and still respectful manner, and then remove yourself from the situation or organization involved. If your disagreement is due to legal reasons, you also have an obligation to report to appropriate law enforcement officials.

Sometimes we need to just let go and move on.

Sometimes it is helpful to take and record a moral inventory of your life and actions to include how you may have hurt or offended others. If you do this, speak with a trusted friend or counselor on how to proceed with this information. Making amends when possible is important, apologizing is important, but never push this onto a past victim when it is illegal or unwelcome. There are ways to do this when needed and a good counselor can help. The most important thing here is helping you let go and move on; and when and where appropriate, make amends for past mistakes.

> "Happiness is like a butterfly; the more you chase it, the more it will elude you, but if you turn your attention to other things, it will come and sit softly on your shoulder."
> - Henry David Thoreau

Anger and violence can both be addictive, and are often associated with many kinds of addictions. In the addiction recovery groups my wife and I facilitate, I often hear great wisdom gained through years of difficult and often heart wrenching experiences. Recently, one of them said in a meeting that 'as an addict, we do not have the luxury of contention, resentment or anger.' Truly the same can be said of anyone.

> When appropriate and needed, Alcoholics Anonymous or another 12 Step Program, as well as other similar programs can help.
> http://weight-lossnewsandresearch.blogspot.com/2017/09/forgiveness-and-stress-research.html

Let go and learn better ways to manage disappointments, stress, and conflict.

> http://weight-lossnewsandresearch.blogspot.com/2017/09/anger-and-addiction.html
>
> http://weight-lossnewsandresearch.blogspot.com/2017/09/violence-and-addiction.html

> "I believe that love and forgiveness engages an incomprehensible healing force and sometimes true healing occurs, but always an emotional and spiritual healing happens." — Angeli Maun Akey
>
> "It's so important to realize that every time you get upset, it drains your emotional energy. Losing your cool makes you tired. Getting angry a lot messes with your health." - Joyce Meyer
>
> "The best attribute a believer can have is forgiveness." Hasan Al-Basri

Yes, there is hypocrisy all around. I and everyone else I know is far from perfect. Let it go. Live your life to the very best of your ability. Get good help if you need it. Make positive changes you need to make and continue to progress. Choose health, life, and, love.

Be slow to judge and quick to love. Good advice for a better life.

> "To be a Christian means to forgive the inexcusable because God has forgiven the inexcusable in you." — C.S. Lewis
>
> "Forgiveness is an act of the will, and the will can function regardless of the temperature of the heart." — Corrie ten Boom
>
> "Forgiveness is not an occasional act, it is a constant attitude." — Martin Luther King Jr.
>
> "Better than a thousand hollow words is one word that brings peace." - Buddha
>
> "The one who pursues revenge should dig two graves." Chinese Proverb
>
> "Always let your talent do the talking. Never your tantrums." – Rasheed Ogunlaru
>
> "People have to forgive. We don't have to like them, we don't have to be friends with them, we don't have to send them hearts in text messages, but we have to forgive them, to overlook, to forget. Because if we don't we are tying rocks to our feet, too much for our wings to carry!" — C. JoyBell C.

18. Learn and practice techniques of hand warming for relaxation.

With practice, it is an easy skill to learn. In your relaxing place, perhaps listening to relaxing music, imagine your hands and fingers warming. If you have a thermometer you can measure your success by taping it to the end of your finger with medical tape. Some of the electronic thermometers are great for this. Think of a relaxing time and place and just let go of any current troubles. Remember, you cannot let go of something without replacing it with something else, make sure you replace with something better. Think of a relaxing time and/or place. Memorize and repeat in your mind a comforting poem, song, or scripture.

19. Get involved with something personally meaningful, positive, and productive.

Volunteer, even if for only a few hours a month. This will help build relationships, positive pride, a sense of accomplishment, and self-efficacy. Sometimes volunteering to help other less fortunate than you, even in very inconspicuous and anonymous ways can provide wonderful lasting benefit for you as well as others you might serve in even the simplest of ways. Everyone has something to give. I have worked most of my life with people with disabilities. I have a fond memory of a conversation I once had with someone who had a disability and who lived in an institution. That simple conversation remains one of the best gifts I have received in my life.

> "Let no one ever come to you without leaving better and happier. Be the living expression of God's kindness—kindness in your face, kindness in your eyes, kindness in your smile, kindness in your warm greeting." – Mother Teresa

20: LOVE

Love and serve others.

Love with good appropriate boundaries and without being a doormat.

Note: Neither violence, nor swearing is mentioned anywhere in this book as stress reduction or stress management techniques. Both increase stress for everyone involved. They may seem, just like the music of Metallica did for my young friend, to reduce stress for the moment, but they are not the path to health.

Remember, the opposite of Love is Fear. (Read: *Love is Letting Go of Fear* by Gerald G. Jampolsky, MD, and **"Perfect Love Casteth Out Fear" 1 John 4:18**) Anger is often a manifestation of Fear.

There are four appropriate and healthy ways to deal with Anger:

1. As described in ABCDE of Rational Emotive Therapy, examine and rethink your feelings and interpretation of events. Use good critical thinking and try some patience and humility.

http://weight-lossnewsandresearch.blogspot.com/2017/09/abcde-of-rational-emotive-therapy.html

2. Talk it out and process in a loving and civil dialogue with the person with whom you are angry.

3. Report to the appropriate authorities if needed.

4. Just let it go.

Be slow to judge and quick to love. Good advice for a better life.

Only in extreme situations should you or anyone need to take more assertive protective actions. Physical aggression is rarely the answer.

While keeping our default future in our remembrance can be an important motivator. The most important motivator will always be associated with health, life, & love.

> "It is true that fear can have a powerful influence over our actions and behavior. But that influence tends to be temporary and shallow. ... People who are fearful may say and do the right things, but they do not feel the right things. They often feel helpless and resentful, even angry." Dieter F. Uchtdorf

Love of life, love of family, love of others, etc.

There is a great book written a few decades ago: _Love, Medicine and Miracles: Lessons Learned about Self-Healing from a Surgeon's Experience with Exceptional Patients_: by Bernie Siegel. In the book Dr. Siegel talks about a woman in the hospital due to lung cancer. He walks in on her and finds her smoking. She puts down the cigarette and says: "I suppose you're going to tell me to stop smoking." Dr. Siegel responds: "No, I'm going to tell you to love yourself and when you do, you'll stop smoking." While there is some truth to this, loving yourself is not enough, but is extremely important.

Love and serve others, forgive others and forgive yourself. If you do not already, as you work do these things; hopefully, you will come to love yourself more.

> "Happiness is the meaning and the purpose of life, the whole aim and end of human existence" - Aristotle.

If you want to find opportunities to serve, you can check out: https://www.justserve.org/

> "If you want more joy in your daily life, smile at the people you meet in the street, the woman sitting beside you on the bus or standing next to you in the queue at the airport, the waiter who brings your food, your colleagues or your employer. There's a great chance they'll smile back." — Thorbjörg Hafsteinsdottir, _10 Years Younger in 10 Weeks_

> "Love people, not things; use things, not people." — Spencer W. Kimball

21. PRAYER and FAITH

Many find great power, solace, and comfort through prayer. Some would be surprised of the power and health benefits derived from prayer, faith, and religion.

There are many scholarly articles on the impact of prayer and faith on stress reduction and health. You can go to your favorite search engine and do a search with the words: prayer, faith, stress.

> You can also go to the following pages and click on the link for scholarly articles on the subjects.
>
> http://weight-lossnewsandresearch.blogspot.com/2017/08/health-stress-prayer-faith.html
>
> http://weight-lossnewsandresearch.blogspot.com/2017/09/religion-and-stress-reduction.html
>
> http://weight-lossnewsandresearch.blogspot.com/2017/09/prayer-and-stress-reduction.html
>
> http://weight-lossnewsandresearch.blogspot.com/2017/09/faith-and-stress-

Recently, one of the men in one of the addiction recovery groups, made a profound comment about the first two steps of the program. His summarization was; "I can't (by myself), He can!"

reduction.html

22. Practice Good Sleep Hygiene.

Get enough, but not too much sleep. At least once a week, allow yourself to stay in bed until you naturally wake up without an alarm of some kind.

Set a sleep schedule and keep it within ½ hour every night of the week; except for one or two nights when you may stay up a little, but not a lot later. If you must work a rotating shift schedule, keep a schedule according to your shift. (Rotating work schedules have their problems and should be avoided when possible.) Keeping a regular schedule helps condition your body to expect sleep at certain times. Young children can have naps, infants must have frequent naps and toddlers should have naps. Children should stick with the same schedule, within a ½ hour variance as much as possible seven days a week.

* "Early to bed, early to rise." There is a lot of wisdom in the adage. Even though some people are just not morning people, for some, this can help their sleep patterns.

* Avoid sleeping too much or too little. At least a couple of times a week you should stay in bed until you wake up without an alarm, and then don't just lie in bed. Again, you want to condition your body and mind that the bed is for sleeping, not just lying around.

* Bed is for sleeping and for adults, certain pleasurable activities, nothing else. Do not watch TV in bed. Do not be on your computer in bed. Do not talk on the phone in bed. Do not use your smart phone in bed, etc. Do not read in bed. You want the primary cue to your brain and body when you go to bed to be SLEEP! Never underestimate the power of natural cues, (music, TV, telephone, computer, etc.) that tell a child or an adult that it's time to sleep or time to play or be involved in some other activity. You want the cues associated with being in bed to be all about going to sleep.

* Do not watch TV in your bedroom or use it as an office or for a computer room. This is also part of conditioning your mind and body.

* Avoid stimulants such as caffeine and nicotine. Remember chocolate and many sodas have caffeine. (If you eat or drink chocolate or use other stimulants, do not do so within 4 hours of going to bed.)

* Keep refined sugar or high fructose corn syrup to a minimum and do not consume either within 4 hours of going to bed. Eliminating them is best.

* Avoid alcohol, while it may help you to get to sleep, it will make it more difficult to get a good night's sleep.

* Sleep in a cool (not cold) room and warm (not hot) comfortable bed. Try wearing socks to bed (unless your feet are too hot) and in extreme situations where you have chronically cold hands, try mittens. Your body needs to regulate your temperature, often warming your hands and feet, before you can get to sleep.

* Keep up a good exercise routine, but not within two hours of bedtime. Stretching, yoga, and deep breathing, can be helpful right before bed.

* Create a relaxing bedtime routine and stick with it. This can last from 30 minutes to an hour. It can include stretching, yoga, a warm bath, deep breathing, and reading (not in the bedroom). Avoid stressful activities and conversations right before going to bed or in bed.

* Do Not eat a large meal within 4 hours of going to bed. Light snack, right before bed, i.e.., warm milk, banana, white cheese, walnuts, may be helpful for some. Avoid spicy food right before bed and possibly discontinue altogether if it causes you an upset stomach. If you are a food addict or binge eater, avoid eating in the evening.

* Make sure you get good exposure to natural light. People, who do not get outside often, are helped by getting the sunlight through the window. Natural light helps to maintain a healthy sleep cycle.

* Eliminate light and distracting noise as much as possible while sleeping. Sometimes quiet relaxing music or relaxing nature sounds can be helpful. Sometimes a comforting sound from the past can also be helpful. I find the light sound of a distant train very relaxing. If you enjoy it, baroque music is very conducive to a good night's sleep. Use specific sounds or music associated with sleep only for when you are falling asleep.

* Do Not ruminate over issues that cause you stress right before or at bedtime. Think about something pleasant. If you cannot do this on your own, listen to some pleasant music or watch some good positive comedy (but not in the bedroom). It is ok to listen to relaxing music while in bed but not television. Don't even have a TV in the bedroom. If you are ruminating about something that needs to be resolved or discussed, and if it is possible to do so, talk it out peacefully well before going to bed.

* If you do everything or most of the things mentioned here and do not fall asleep within 20 to 25 minutes, get up and do something relaxing for 30 to 45 minutes and then try again. If you wake up in the night and do not fall back to sleep within 20 to 25 minutes, get up and do something relaxing for 30 to 45 minutes. (You may want to go into another room and read.)

* Consult with your physician if you have chronic sleep problems or chronic pain that keeps you awake. If you are taking medications, speak with your physician about possible side effects that may cause sleep problems.

* Some scents have been found helpful for both relaxing and falling asleep. You may want to try some good quality scented oils (don't use the type that requires fire or high heat as falling asleep and fire or high heat can be very dangerous). Try lavender, jasmine, valerian, and rose (only try one at a time and see if it helps.

For foods, herbal teas, and scents, try one thing at a time. See what happens then try something else. Use scents that are safe for you and for children and don't burn a candle overnight or where children have access. Trying one thing at a time is a basic scientific method and will help you better understand what works for you.

One common problem for some children is trying to get them to sleep too much. Some children become non-nappers at an early age, and trying to get them to nap and then go to sleep a few hours later may not work well. (Infants and babies need a lot of sleep.)

Relaxing music, such as baroque, some country, and other music can also be very helpful, especially if it is only used when going to sleep. This provides an additional cue to your brain that it's time to sleep. For young children, my favorite is: <u>When you Wish Upon a Star</u> by Daniel Kobialka.

Another thing you may try with young children, is to play music as mentioned above that is only played at bedtime and perhaps while they are asleep. You can also try blowing big bubbles. Very quietly, blow big bubbles with your child or children. As children blow large bubbles they must breathe deeply, which changes their physiology to a more relaxed state. Try a couple times along with your regular routine, and the music, to see what happens. If it helps, great, if not, you've had an enjoyable activity with your child.

If none of these things work for children, and they want to be with you or to do something else, consider what they are getting from not going to sleep, or what they are getting out of by not going to sleep (secondary gain)? This is another basic concept of behaviorism. You may also want to find out if there are any fears involved. Perhaps the child has a recurring nightmare. If none of this helps and it is a severe problem, consult their physician.

While lying in bed, you can try deep and slow breathing. Lying on your back; breathe in through your nose and out through your mouth. As you do this, tighten muscles as you breathe in and relax as you breathe out. Start at your feet and push down in the bed as you are breathing in and relax as you are breathing out. Move up to your calves and do the same. Do this all the way up your body and finish with your head, push down as you breathe in and relax as you breathe out.

One of my favorite techniques is to breathe slowly, paying attention to my breathing and my heart beat and counting my heart beat as I slowly and deeply breathe in and out. I pay close attention to my heartbeat as it slows to a more relaxed rhythm. Most of the time when I do this, I'm soon asleep.

Avoid sleeping pills if possible. If necessary, consult your physician.

* Even if you do not get a good night's sleep, get up at your scheduled time. If you get less than 4 hours of sleep for three nights in a row or less than 2 hours of sleep for two nights in a row, consult your physician. If you sleep, but do not feel rested on a chronic basis, even after you have tried these adjustments, consult your physician. You may have a serious sleep disorder such as apnea.

Some healthier foods that can help sleep:

> Good sleep hygiene and patterns help enhance weight loss.
> http://weight-lossnewsandresearch.blogspot.com/2017/12/weight-loss-sleep-circadian-rhythm.html

Almonds, Bananas, Barley (Rolled, it's easy to cook by just putting some in a bowl, adding water so that it is just above the barley, and then putting it in the microwave. Start with 1 minute), Cheese (white, to include cottage cheese), Cherries (on the tart side is best for sleeping), Chickpeas, Kale, Lettuce, Milk, Oats (Rolled, you can cook oats or barley on the stove or in the microwave as described above. Rolled oats may help some to wake and others to sleep better), Rice (Brown), Tuna, Turkey (While turkey may help. Some of these other foods are likely to help more, and the greatest sleep benefit of the turkey comes in combination with other foods such as the grains and white cheese.), Walnuts, Yogurt (no sugar)

If any of these foods are gateway foods, foods that once you eat them you feel an urge to eat more of that food or other foods, then don't eat them right before bed. If you are a food addict or binge eater, do not eat in the evening. Being tired and/or stressed make it more difficult to replace bad habits with good.

Scents that can help you sleep (remember, no candles, no fire)

Chamomile, Frankincense, Jasmine, Lavender, Mandarin, Sandalwood

Of course, physical hygiene and sanitation are also crucial for good health.

> For research, go to these web pages:
> http://weight-lossnewsandresearch.blogspot.com/2017/08/sleep-hygiene.html
> http://weight-lossnewsandresearch.blogspot.com/2017/11/alzheimers-and-sleep-deprivation.html

First Step

Start your day after a good restful sleep.

Second Step

http://weight-lossnewsandresearch.blogspot.com/2017/09/alzheimers-prevention-sleep.html

Choos

http://weight-lossnewsandresearch.blogspot.com/2017/09/weight-loss-sleep.html

e one area where you believe you need to and can easily make a change, with or without help. Get the help you need and set a goal and the steps/objectives to make the change. (Goals and objectives will be discussed later.)

Remember, always address risks of self-harm or harm to others immediately and with the proper authorities or resources according to where you live.

LET'S REVIEW

THE FOUNDATION

| STRESS MANAGEMENT/SLEEP |
| EXERCISE: AEROBIC & STRENGTH/RESISTANCE |
| **FOOD SECURITY** |

Establishing *The Foundation*, early, daily, will expand your physical, emotional, and mental capacity.

Note: This is only the foundation.

Essential HABITS, and TOOLS, are also crucial forhealthy, sustainablee weight loss, and overcoming addictions.

When you build and then maintain this foundation daily, eliminating the crap, not only does it make it easier to overcome a food addiction, but any addiction. And, research has shown that up to 75% of all medical visits and prescriptions can be safely eliminated for most people if they incorporate this type of healthy lifestyle. Never stop a medication without the consent of your doctor. Continue to meet with your doctor as recommended.

Go to this link to learn how diet and exercise can help reduce the need and cost of medical visits:

http://quickhealthymealsonabudget.blogspot.com/2017/08/diet-and-exercise-can-help-reduce.html

"The best six doctors anywhere

And no one can deny it

Are sunshine, water, rest, and air

Exercise and diet.

These six will gladly you attend

If only you are willing

Your mind they'll ease

Your will they'll mend

And charge you not a shilling."

-- Nursery rhyme quoted by Wayne Fields, <u>What the River Knows</u>, 1990"

The Foundation allows you to be more:

Reflective, and less

Reactive and Reflexive: (Changing bad habits to good can be done, but takes time and consistent effort.)

Habits are learned and controlled by the Basal ganglia. This is a part of what is called the old brain. This is important because it allows us to be more efficient. Perhaps you have driven somewhere you often go and when you arrived, realized you didn't remember the trip. While this is not safe and we need to be mindful and pay attention when we drive, the reason is simple, habits. We do all kinds of activities, both good and bad because of habits which are controlled by the Basal ganglia. When you drive a car, there are many things you do without thinking. You change how much pressure you have on the accelerator, you may shift and slightly turn without really thinking.

This is important because it allows you to pay attention and notice the child who may run into the road, or other potential dangers.

Much of our eating and drinking is due to habits, some good and some... perhaps mostly for some of us, bad habits. This book teaches you new, good habits which will help you be healthier and if needed, lose weight. Even when we are trying to make better choices, old habits often kick in. Habits and the basal ganglia have more power over us when we are tired, stressed (to include sick), and under the influence of alcohol and many types of drugs. Extra diligence, greater effort, and better planning must be used in these situations. Helpful skills, techniques, and habits are taught throughout this book.

In my case, I have changed many, if not most, of my old unhealthy eating habits, but under more stressful situations, I can still slip back into some of my old bad habits. When this occurs, such as recently after moving, I've had to adjust. In this case I had to stop purchasing even healthy peanut butter for a while because I would eat some in the middle of the night when I would get up to use the restroom. At this point in my life, I just can't have it around. There are foods and drink, which may fall under the **Good**, or **Better**, or even **Best** category, which when you are tired, under stress, or under the influence of drugs or alcohol, you must avoid. These may be foods and drinks which are personal "gateway foods." Gateway goods are those which once you eat them you lose control. You may eat too much of that food or they may seem to compel you to eat or drink something you should not---or just a lot more than you should or need.

This is individual. There are some people who cannot eat in the evening because they cannot or have great difficulty stopping. There are gateway foods that, on an individual basis, can be eaten in the morning but not in the evening. There are also gateway foods which simply cannot be eaten at all or must be eaten rarely. For example: I love a good potato salad. I also love a good deviled egg. In the categories of Poor, Good, Better, and Best, I would place both under the good column. The problem is that I absolutely love both and tend to lose control. If someone at work has a great deviled egg and I eat even one, I am likely to come home and eat a lot of other foods, perhaps also in the good or better category, but over-eat all the same. (There is someone at my work who makes amazing deviled eggs.) Even if I eat a good potato salad at breakfast, I am likely to blow it the rest of the day. This doesn't mean I NEVER eat potato salad, but about twice a year is enough if I want to stay in my target weight range and in good health. I have come to discover that there are simply things more important to me than potato salad. You may also have to decide that things like health, life, and loved ones, are more important to you than certain personal gateway foods or drinks. (There is a recipe towards the end of this book for a mock potato salad using cauliflower, which is surprisingly good.)

Much of this is individual, which is the reason personal data is so important. As you record the data discussed later in the book, you will come to better understand your strengths and limitations. With this data, and the support of others, including programs mentioned in this book, you will come to understand personal adjustments you need to make.

The foundation helps us make better choices because it helps clear our mind, satisfy our nutritional needs, and reduce stress. The foundation makes the rest of the journey easier, but not easy. It will require work and at times it will be difficult. On occasion, I still must ask myself the question: "What matters most to me?" My answer is: **Health, Life, and Love**.

> "Every Worthy Act Is Difficult. Ascent Is Always Difficult. Descent Is Easy and Often Slippery" – Mahatma Gandhi
>
> "If you want to be strong challenge yourself to something that makes you feel weak." — Toni Sorenson
>
> If you always do what you've always done, you'll always get what you've always got.
>
> Perhaps the greatest human quest: is for self-mastery and personal evolution.

Healthy people, with the requisite skills, tend to understand and have the ability to appropriately respond to the difference between needs and wants.

> It is NOT too late to begin!
>
> "You are never too old to set a new goal or dream a new dream." CS Lewis
>
> "The best time to plant a tree was 20 years ago. The second-best time is now." – Chinese Proverb
>
> "If we are creating ourselves all the time, then it is never too late to begin creating the bodies we want instead of the ones we mistakenly assume we are stuck with." — Deepak Chopra
>
> Even if you fail 1000 times, it's getting up; it's failing forward that matters most.

The changes discussed here; the habits, skills, and techniques I am teaching in this book are not complicated but they are also not easy. It will take effort, but I hope I've presented this in a way that will help you understand and be able to make the changes needed to substantially improve your health. This is not to replace your doctor or needed medication, but, under medical supervision, you may find your need for medical care and medication at least partially diminished. Never discontinue a medication unless under the supervision and with the support and permission of your doctor or licensed medical practitioner. All the medication I stopped using was in consultation with my doctor. Remember, just take baby steps. This isn't a sprint.

Like me, you may be motivated and may have been motivated in the past; but while motivation is crucial, it's not enough.

Begin your day by establishing *The Foundation*. Start your day with Food Security and Aerobic Exercise after having had a good night's Sleep. This will help reduce unhealthy **cravings**, improve mental clarity, improve energy (over time), improve personal capacity, and make you more Reflexive and less Reactive. This will be true for almost anyone.

> "People often say that motivation doesn't last. Neither does bathing that's why we recommend it daily." Zig Ziggler
>
> "Success is the sum of small efforts, repeated day in and day out." – Robert Collier
>
> If you have questions and need additional support, you can ask here: https://www.facebook.com/DeliciousNutritionStealthHealth/
>
> "Though no one can go back and make a brand-new start, anyone can start from now and make a brand new ending." Carl Bard
>
> "When everything seems to be going against you, remember that the airplane takes off against the wind, not with it." Henry Ford

This book will be best used as a resource and workbook while participating in a support group or class.

Many years ago, when I was a child and family therapist, I took a group of 5 young men to scout camp for a week. These young men did

> "Appetite has really become an artificial and abnormal thing, having taken the place of true hunger, which alone is natural. The one is a sign of bondage but the other, of freedom." — Paul Brunton, The Notebooks of Paul Brunton

not have The Foundation. They were typically much more reactive than reflexive. Anger, violence, and homelessness, were the norm in their lives. I believed the experience camping would be good for them. I was also very concerned about their behavior, and how I would help maintain peace between them, and the hundred or so other boys at camp. To my surprise, they had no stamina. By the time they were finished with the day's activities, they were exhausted. They were the first to get into their sleeping bags and fall asleep. The Foundation, the whole foundation can be like the difference between night and day, between manure and clean water.

The minimal required to establish food security in the morning is 2 servings of whole grain, 2 servings of vegetables (limit starchy vegetables) 1 serving of fruit and 1 serving of protein (plant based, including all the essential amino acids is best). Don't forget water. Consult with your physician if you have diabetes.

Brown rice and beans are considered by most a complete protein. Quinoa is also considered a complete protein by most experts. Other good sources of protein are:

For information on essential amino acids (protein) go to the following webpage: http://weight-lossnewsandresearch.blogspot.com/2017/08/essential-amino-acids-protein.html

Almonds, Asparagus, **Broccoli**, Cauliflower, **Chia Seeds**, **Peanuts**, **Pumpkin Seeds**, Spinach, <u>**Walnuts**</u>

I like to make homemade bread that has a lot of protein. I have a wheat grinder, but know a lot of people who grind wheat with a coffee grinder.

My wife tries to eat gluten free so I make two similar recipes.

Grind 4 cups of either wheat or brown rice. While grinding, I also grind ¼ cup quinoa and ¼ cup Chia seeds. This will make about 7 cups of flour. You can also make this bread with ¼ cup Chia seeds, ¼ cup quinoa and 6 ½ cups whole wheat, oat, or brown rice flour, if you are not able to grind your own flour. You can leave the Chia seeds and quinoa unground.

In a mixer, I pour 4 cups of **hot** water.

Add the 7 cups wheat or brown rice flour mixed with the quinoa and Chia seeds and mix briefly. This is a total of 7 cups with the quinoa and Chia seeds mixed in.

Add 2 large eggs and mix.

Next, I add 1 tablespoon of salt, ½ cup olive or avocado oil and ½ cup honey. (As you can see there are lots of calories here and plenty of healthy fat.)

Add ¼ cup potato starch and ¼ cup flaxseed meal.

Mix again.

Add:

1 tablespoon salt

1 teaspoon baking soda

1 teaspoon baking powder

> Mix
>
> Add:
>
> 1 tablespoon dry yeast
>
> Mix well
>
> You do not need to knead. This will be similar to thick cake dough.
>
> Pour the mixture into two or three bread pans, sprayed with butter flavored spray oil. Two large bread pans or three medium sized pans. (You don't want it to spill over as it rises.)
>
> Cover and let rise for 20 minutes (but no more). I place the bread pans with the rising dough on top of the stove with the oven heating which makes it a bit warmer for rising.
>
> Place in an oven preheated to 325 for 60 minutes. (This can vary depending on the oven and altitude. Check to make sure it's done by sticking a fork or table knife in. If it comes out clean, is is probably done.)
>
> Take out and let cool, enjoy. Store in the refrigerator.

Your body and mind are a completely integrated system. If you attack (poison) or neglect one part of the system, you weaken the whole.

The Healthy Side of Cravings

Most of the time when I talk about cravings in this book, they have a negative connotation. For most in the United States and much of the world, cravings have been degraded and corrupted, and they are exactly as described throughout this book. For many people who have succumbed to poor eating habits, it will be difficult to bring back and get in touch with their natural healthy cravings. My experience is mixed. Sometimes I still crave crap, but most of the time I now crave healthy foods. Fortunately, I have come to know the difference.

> "We can, and must, develop dialogue and relatedness with our body because it's talking to us all the time. And please remember, your body loves you. It does everything it can to keep you alive and functioning. You can feed it garbage, and it will take it and digest it for you. You can deprive it of sleep, but still it gets you up and running next morning. You can drink too much alcohol, and it will eliminate it from your system. It loves you unconditionally and does its best to allow you to live the life you came here for. The real issue in this relationship is not whether your body loves you, but whether you love your body. In any

When I crave something that is healthy, if it is within my calorie and fat budget, I will add it to my diet in the next day or two. For example, not too long ago I was really craving a brown rice, bean, and vegetable soup I sometimes make. I've made it a couple times in the past month and my mind and body loves it. It's cheap and easy to make. I'll tell you quickly how to make it.

> relationship, if one partner is loving, faithful and supportive, it's easy for the other to take that person for granted. That's what most of us do with our bodies. It is time for you to shift this, and working to understand your cravings is one of the best places to begin. Then you can build a mutually loving relationship with your own body." — Joshua Rosenthal, <u>Integrative Nutrition: Feed Your Hunger for Health and Happiness</u>

Back to the recipe: Pour into a pot with a lid (pressure cooker is best but not necessary) one cup dry beans of your choice and one cup brown rice. (Sometimes I will add one cup dry peas or lentils too.) Add water until it is at least an inch over the top of the rice and beans. Put the lid on and let it sit overnight.

The next day: Add water until there is 2 inches of water on top of the beans and rice (and dry peas or lentils if they were added).

Put on the stove with lid on and turn to medium high.

Bring to a hard boil.

Turn down to low and let simmer for 15 minutes.

Let cool and carefully pour off the excess water.

Put back on stove and add 3 cups water.

Turn burner on stove up to medium high.

Add one can of broth. I usually use vegetable broth.

Add one can of corn or green beans, include the liquid in the can.

Add one large chopped onion.

Add one chopped potato.

Add one chopped large bell pepper or if you like it a little hot, add another pepper (or two or three) of your choice.

If you can get them, I do from my garden in the summer, add a cup of chopped green tomatoes. You can use tomatoes from the store, but they are not as good.

Add a cup chopped zucchini.

You may also want to add some greens and or cabbage. The last time I made this I added cut up beet greens and it was delicious.

Add 1 tablespoon cumin or better yet, cumin seeds.

Add 1 tablespoon salt.

2 or 3 chopped cloves of garlic.

Another optional ingredient is a can of olives, sliced and the liquid also poured into the mix.

Typically, I add the hardest vegetable first and the softest last. This allows the harder vegetables longer cooking time. I stir in between each that I add. For example, if I would use a red cabbage, I would have that chopped and add it first and in this example, I would add the beet greens last.

Bring to a boil and allow it to simmer until done. After everything has been added and it comes to a boil, turn it to low, put the lid back on and let it simmer for at least another 15 minutes. How long you need to let it simmer will depend on the type of beans you're using.

Some people may like to add a little cayenne pepper. My wife likes to add black pepper and garlic.

If you include all the ingredients listed above, you have: Whole grains, Vegetables, Fruit, and all the essential amino acids (protein). If you eat a good serving, you will have food security (for the day you eat it).

While losing weight I had a simple shake I would drink every other morning. Here's the recipe.

In a blender, add:

One cup rolled oats

1 banana

1 cup milk (I used to use powdered milk or 2%. Now I use almond milk)

1 scoop protein powder (pea is considered by many to be healthier)

2 large chopped carrots or 10 baby carrots.

1 tablespoon virgin organic coconut oil

1 tablespoon Ceylon cinnamon

1/3 cup stevia (in the raw/granules, not liquid)

1 cup water

Blend

    Add ice, depending on the quality of your blender, you may want to add just a little ice, blend, and then add a little more and blend again until you have what you want. For all my smoothies or shakes you can drink them all for breakfast, leave some for later, or share. Also, for all my shakes and smoothies, if you have diabetes, try just one cup first. Test yourself and see how you respond.

For a simple variation on the above smoothie which is one of my grandchildren's favorites, add 2 tablespoons natural unsweetened peanut butter and 2 tablespoons unsweetened powdered baking chocolate.

3 great things about this shake are:

1. Food Security
2. Physically filling (It looks like you are getting a lot more calories than you are, though you are getting plenty of calories.)
3. Psychologically filling

Cinnamon is especially good for blood sugar and if you use cinnamon regularly, the Ceylon is a better health choice. Quite often people with diabetes are advised to avoid bananas; however, food combinations matter. In this case you are consuming it with complex carbohydrates and protein. If you have diabetes and want to try this, drink just one cup, then test your blood sugar levels after, and repeat to verify levels and the effect it may have on you personally. If it raises your blood sugar more than it would normally rise after eating, discontinue. Also, consult with your physician before trying and follow the advice of your physician.

This smoothie is a great way to start the day and you may want to add something like two pieces of whole wheat toast without anything additional added. Even if you get incredible results from this smoothie, and some will, you do not want to eat the same thing every day. Healthy variety is important for a wide variety of important nutrients.

http://weight-lossnewsandresearch.blogspot.com/2017/12/diabetes-and-myplate.html

http://weight-lossnewsandresearch.blogspot.com/2017/12/diabetes-and-food-combinations.html

Here is another very healthy smoothie:

Add to a blender:

Two large washed stalks of rhubarb cut into small pieces

Two cups frozen strawberries

Two large carrots, cut into small pieces or 10 baby carrots

1 scoop vanilla protein

1 tablespoon Ceylon cinnamon

1 cup milk (I prefer almond)

2 cups water

½ cup stevia, in granules or in the raw (Anytime when stevia is mentioned you may want more or less than I have listed. Add according to your taste.)

1 cup old fashioned rolled oats or rolled barley

Blend well. As with all the smoothies, if you have a cheaper blender, you may need to blend after each time you add an ingredient and start with the milk and water. If you use frozen strawberries, no ice is needed. If you use fresh strawberries you may want to add some ice.

Here is another I really like:

Add to a blender:

1 sweet potato, cut into small pieces, washed and with any bad parts removed. (Some people call these yams, but what I use are orange. Leave the peel on the potato.)

1 cup old fashioned rolled oats

1 cup milk (I prefer almond)

1 cup water

2 large cored apples, washed, cut into small pieces and with the peel still on the apple.

1 tablespoon pumpkin pie spice (you may prefer a little less)

½ cup stevia granules or powder

1 scoop vanilla protein (I prefer pea)

Blend well and if you have a cheaper blender, you may need to blend a little each time you add a new ingredient and start with the milk and water.

Add ice, again, you may need to add a little at a time and blend each time.

This is quite delicious and another great way to start your day. If too much to drink for breakfast, save some for lunch. If you need to chew something, have a couple pieces of whole wheat toast. If you don't have enough time to make this in the morning, like all my smoothies, you can make it in the evening, put in the refrigerator overnight, add ice in the morning, and drink.

While this next one was not the smoothie I mostly used as I was losing weight, it is now one I make and drink often. This may sound crazy, but as your taste changes, you may find this quite good and both physically and psychologically satisfying. This is the smoothie I call my **Anti-Alzheimers, anti-Cancer, and anti-Diabetes smoothie**. It is not guaranteed to prevent any of these, but contains many ingredients that may help.

Add to a large and good quality blender:

1 cup old fashioned rolled oats or rolled barley

2 large carrots (for all carrots in all the recipes, wash well, cut off the ends, but do not peel) or 10 baby carrots.

1 stalk celery (I cut off the ends, be sure and wash)

About 2-3 inches of fresh cucumber, washed and with the skin sill on. (Cucumbers, strawberries, and walnuts may be good for memory.)

1 cup milk (I prefer almond)

2 cups water

¼ cup walnuts

¼ cup unsweetened dried cranberries

1 cardamom pod

2 small sheets of seaweed or ½ large sheet (You want to end up with about half the size of a piece of typing paper. I hate seaweed but they are one of the most nutritious foods on the planet and you can't taste it in this.)

1 teaspoon turmeric

1 tablespoon virgin organic coconut oil

4 tablespoons powdered unsweetened baking chocolate

1 tablespoon Ceylon cinnamon

1 banana

1 scoop chocolate protein (pea is generally considered healthier)

1/3 cup stevia in the raw/granules

Blend well. Add ice and blend again.

There is some research which shows that this type of diet MAY be **helpful** to prevent cancer. You can find information on one if the ingredients, turmeric, and cancer here:

http://weight-lossnewsandresearch.blogspot.com/2017/08/turmeric-and-cancer.html

Many of the ingredients in this smoothie may be helpful for memory; you can find information on strawberries, cucumbers, and memory here:

http://weight-lossnewsandresearch.blogspot.com/2017/08/strawberries-cucumbers-and-memory.html

For information about walnuts for memory or weight loss, go here:

http://weight-lossnewsandresearch.blogspot.com/2017/08/walnuts-and-memory-and-weight-loss.html

You can find many variations here: http://quickhealthymealsonabudget.blogspot.com/

Since I brought up walnuts, I'll share one more recipe here which is delicious. I've shared this with one of my classes and they loved it, one person said it was the best salad he had ever had.

Wilted spinach salad

Start with about 6 cups of loosely packed baby spinach in a large bowl.

In a frying pan, fry five pieces of bacon, cut into small pieces. Do not fry until crisp. (I eat meat very sparingly. I eat bacon, even more rarely. This dish and my incredibly delicious quiche are almost the only exceptions. Bacon comes under the "crap" category, but I add it here for the taste. Bacon bits may work just as well.)

(As noted previously, I'm not a vegetarian; however, here is a quote worth including: "I don't understand why asking people to eat a well-balanced vegetarian diet is considered drastic, while it is medically conservative to cut people open and put them on cholesterol lowering drugs for the rest of their lives." — Dean Ornish)

Back to the recipe: Remove the outer peel and thinly slice 4 onions. Sautee the onions in a pan sprayed with canned spray oil. Before the onions are completely sautéed, add ¼ cup crushed walnuts and ½ cup quinoa to the sautéed onions. Continue to stir. Add the bacon, without the excess grease, to the onions, walnuts, and quinoa. Continue to stir until the bacon is crisper.

Also, in a pot, hard boil 4 large eggs. When hard boiled, pour off the water, add cold water, then when the eggs have cooled enough to handle, peel the eggs and slice into about ¼ inch slices.

Add both the sliced eggs and the hot onions, walnuts, and quinoa to the spinach. Toss the salad. The hot ingredients will create the wilted spinach.

Add one can drained and rinsed mandarin oranges.

Serve warm

Note: there is good evidence that eggs should be limited to no more than two or three a week.

5 Habits, 5 Skills and Techniques

This book is based on my own experience and the scientific research of others which allowed me to lose 115+ pounds, after struggling for over 30 years. I am now, even after seven years, able to maintain a healthy weight and lifestyle. The foundation and five habits and skills described in this book have helped me get off medication for diabetes, and almost off medication for high blood pressure. My A1C over the past 7 years has ranged from 4.8 to 5.2. (A1C represents a person's average blood sugar level over the previous 3 months and less than 7.0 is considered good.)

First a little more on Why I Wrote This Book

After losing the weight and going off medication for diabetes I started providing free presentations for local diabetes groups. One of the area diabetes coordinators recommended I write the information from the classes in book form. This is part of the result. Feedback for improvement of this book is always welcome. You can leave comments at: https://www.facebook.com/DeliciousNutritionStealthHealth/. Since writing the first editions of this book which did not include the information on The Foundation, I have continued to teach in the community; however, a few years ago I was trained as a Diabetes Prevention Program (DPP) Lifestyle Coach and have been volunteering to teach those classes. DPP is similar to the changes I made to lose weight and so has been a natural fit. It has been gratifying to see so many lose so much weight over the past few years.

You've seen a picture of me when I was morbidly obese. As mentioned, that picture was terribly embarrassing at the time; however, I am now proud of the picture in relation to the changes I've made. You have seen a more recent picture. This picture is one which was taken after I lost 110 lbs., and before I went on to lose an additional 5 lbs. It was taken in May of 2013.

My original goal was to lose 100 pounds. After losing the 100 pounds I realized I was still considered overweight, according to my body mass index (BMI) which was above 25. I decided to lose another 15 pounds, which brought me to a "normal" weight for the first time since I was a teen. Even as a teen I was only in the "normal" range for a couple of years. Since then my goal has been to stay within 5 pounds of that new low weight. It has not always been easy, I have gone up and down, but stayed within a few pounds of my target weight, getting down to 150 at one point. I currently have a new goal of 148 which will more solidly put me into the normal range for BMI.

Though I share a little about my personal diet and struggle, this book is not about a diet beyond creating a firm and healthy foundation. This is NOT a diet book. There are hundreds of thousands of diets out there. Most of them work, for at least one person, for at least a short period of time. Many or perhaps even most diets you read and hear about are not very healthy and most don't provide you with the required skills, habits, or lifestyle changes, to help you keep it off for the rest of your life. **"Anything that sounds too good to be true probably is. There are no shortcuts to anyplace worth going." - Dave Ramsey** *The Foundation* is not a diet; it is just healthy living. Because establishing the foundation daily, allows many people to eat more, you might even call it an "anti-diet." I am also a behaviorist and weight loss and maintenance as well as healthy eating is as much about behavior, relationships, and environment, as about any specific diet.

The following sections are about healthy, **Habits**, **Skills**, **Tools** and **Techniques**. As you learn and do what is presented in this book, if you need to lose weight, unless there is a medical issue keeping you from losing weight, most of you will lose weight. If you establish the foundation daily, and continue the habits, skills, tools, and techniques, you are very likely to keep the weight off. Many of you will find increased energy and some may even experience improved memory.

As always, if you have significant health problems, consult your licensed medical professional before beginning the changes recommended here.

In the beginning of this book I presented some excuses on why I became obese in-spite of being an active kid. However; I also must take personal responsibility because I developed a sweet tooth and looked for anything delicious I could devour. When my older sister got married, she stored the top of her wedding cake in our freezer to be eaten at their anniversary. At the time, I didn't know the reason. Yes, I found it, and yes, I ate it. I was a fat kid and endured most of the humiliations common to fat kids. Humiliations and teasing I would not wish on any child, teen, or adult. My heart goes out to people who are morbidly obese at any age.

Between my highschool sophomore and junior years I went on a decidedly unhealthy diet, but managed to get myself temporarily into fairly good shape. This lasted until I was about 19 when I slowly started to put it back on. I continued to be physically active, but had again become overweight. I was starting to have symptoms, which I didn't fully understand at the time, of both low blood sugar and depression.

At age 26 I married a beautiful young woman by the name of Jasmine. We went on to have four wonderful children and now have five wonderful grandchildren. As I write this, we have been married for over 34 years. Soon after our marriage, I started to put on more weight to the point of becoming morbidly obese. I continued to walk quite a bit, though, became decidedly less active than I had previously been. At one point, I was prescribed the Fen-Phen drug diet and lost a lot of weight. . . for a while, then put it all back on and a lot more. Of course, I worried about the possible side effects which may have been caused by the medications. Incidentally, there are many very unhealthy thin people. Remember, **if you eat crap, your gunna feel like crap, if not today, eventually**.

I have also had 9 eye surgeries, two on one eye and 7 on the other ending in the loss of one of my eyes. My eye problems impacted my activity level for many years. I vividly remember on July 4th, 1996 while my sons were still quite young, I was trying to play soccer in our back yard with the two of them. I say "trying" because even at their young age, because of my obesity I was no match for either. While trying to play soccer, one of my retinae detached. (While not enjoyable, it was an interesting experience watching my own retina detach.) Because of my eye diagnosis and the complete loss of sight in one eye, I was fearful too much physical exertion would cause the retina in the other eye to detach putting me in another downward spiral to total blindness in my better eye. After many years living under this cloud of fear, I finally decided I could no longer live my life like this. Other ophthalmologists have since told me the chance of another detachment is slim, but either way, I don't want to live my life afraid of physical activity.

Scared of Alzheimer's

As mentioned previously, my father had Alzheimer's and according to an uncle, my grandfather also had Alzheimer's. Having diabetes and being overweight are both huge risk factors for Alzheimer's. For me, Alzheimer's has been a bigger fear than blindness.

Alzheimer's is often referred to as "type 3 diabetes."

Seeing what it did to my father who we cared for, I was highly motivated to avoid Alzheimer's.

"According to the surgeon general, obesity today is officially an epidemic; it is arguably the most pressing public health problem we face, costing the health care system an estimated $90 billion a year. Three of every five Americans are overweight; one of every five is obese. The disease formerly known as adult-onset diabetes has had to be renamed Type II diabetes since it now occurs so frequently in children. A recent study in the Journal of the American Medical Association predicts that a child born in 2000 has a one-in-three chance of developing diabetes. (An African American child's chances are two in five.) Because of diabetes and all the other health problems that accompany obesity, today's children may turn out to be the first generation of Americans whose life expectancy will actually be shorter than that of their parents. The problem is not limited to America: The United Nations reported that in 2000 the number of people suffering from overnutrition--a billion--had officially surpassed the number suffering from malnutrition--800 million." — Michael Pollan, The Omnivore's Dilemma: A Natural History of Four Meals

URL's for two easy to read articles: http://weight-lossnewsandresearch.blogspot.com/2014/09/alzheimers-is-type-3-diabetes-big-think.html

http://scaredofalzheimers.blogspot.com/2012/09/alzheimers-disease-type-3-diabetes-maybe.html

Sometimes URLs are changed and an article may be placed in a different location. If you cannot find the article with the URL, type the name of the article into a search engine and see if it will come up someplace else. In most cases I've tried to avoid that problem by providing a link to my own page which is set up to find the correct articles even if they are moved.

Research:

Diabetes Mellitus and Risk of Alzheimer's Disease and Dementia with Stroke in a Multiethnic Cohort

http://aje.oxfordjournals.org/content/154/7/635.short

Impaired insulin and insulin-like growth factor expression and signaling mechanisms in Alzheimer's disease - *is this type 3 diabetes?*

http://iospress.metapress.com/content/qunmpv4q3w77e5vm/

Increased risk of Alzheimer's disease in Type II diabetes: insulin

Recently a study looked at lifestyle changes that may positively impact Alzheimer's. They found it possible for many to avoid and even reverse Alzheimer's. Those changes are:

1) A mostly vegetarian diet to include what I have identified as Food Security
2) Exercise, with an emphasis on aerobic exercise to include walking
3) Stress management, and
4) A sufficient amount of quality sleep (for adults this is 7-9 hours)

In other words, *The Foundation*!

resistance of the brain or insulin-induced amyloid pathology?

http://europepmc.org/abstract/MED/16246041

Insulin resistance syndrome and Alzheimer's disease: Age- and obesity-related effects on memory, amyloid, and inflammation

http://www.neurobiologyofaging.org/article/S0197-4580(05)00230-7/abstract

Meta-Analysis of Alzheimer's Disease Risk with Obesity, Diabetes, and Related Disorders

http://www.sciencedirect.com/science/article/pii/S0006322309002261

More research on Alzheimer's and Diabetes

http://weight-lossnewsandresearch.blogspot.com/2017/09/alzheimers-and-diabetes.html

Why I Couldn't Lose Weight

The problem was never a lack of motivation. Too often people ascribe the reason someone is fat (or almost any addiction) as simply because they are lazy and/or unmotivated. That may be the case some of the time, but most of the time it is much more complicated and motivation may not even play a part.

http://weight-lossnewsandresearch.blogspot.com/2017/10/reversal-of-cognitive-decline-in.html

http://weight-lossnewsandresearch.blogspot.com/2017/10/alzheimers-and-sleep-deprivation.html

http://weight-lossnewsandresearch.blogspot.com/2017/10/alzheimers-and-exercise.html

http://weight-lossnewsandresearch.blogspot.com/2017/10/alzheimers-and-diet.html

Sometimes there are health issues which keep some from losing weight.

http://weight-lossnewsandresearch.blogspot.com/2017/10/alzheimers-and-vegetarian-diet.html

More often it is because they don't have the habits, skills, knowledge, and tools, to lose the weight and keep it off. Some of the skills and tools they lack may be understanding how to eat healthy on a budget or even what a healthy diet is. Quite often they don't believe they have the power to do anything about the problem. Sometimes it may be the powerful cues from their environment and the people around them. I've often heard the term, "portion control." I have never known anyone who was morbidly obese and who was able to lose weight and keep it off through "portion control" alone. There may be some, but I just haven't known any and it certainly isn't me. For many it would be like telling an alcoholic s/he can manage alcoholism through portion control.

In my case, my continued morbid obesity was caused by a combination of issues. Every time I tried to lose weight and eat less, because of my diabetes, associated blood sugar levels, and intermittent depression, my head would seem to go into a deep fog. I had difficulty concentrating, focusing, and communicating. I have a family to support and couldn't work in that condition. The other problem was I didn't have the **foundation**, **habits, skills, and tools** required to make the critical change needed. I didn't **know** what to do.

Research

When applied wisely, knowledge can be powerful. For many years, and I continue to do this, I read and learned almost everything I could about the following subjects:

1) Alzheimer's: because of my fears, family history, and intense motivation to avoid this disease.
2) Weight Loss, Obesity, and Diabetes: because of my fears and my desire to change.
3) Autism: because of my career.

And all of them because of my love for my family, others, and life. I now LOVE being able to do physical activities I would have never dreamt of doing ten years ago.

While I won't get into it here, there is a strong line of commonality which runs between, Alzheimer's, Obesity, and Diabetes, and even an occasional thin interesting line connecting with some forms of Autism (Autism Spectrum Disorder).

Both of my sons are avid physical fitness and health enthusiasts. (All my children are physically fit.) One provided me with additional research and information on weight loss which turned out to be very helpful.

> For more information on Autism (ASD) visit this page:
> http://parentautismresources.blogspot.com/

As a graduate student in Educational Psychology I took an excellent and extremely demanding class in research and statistics. It was a summer block class and there weren't a lot of class choices. This professor was considered to be the toughest for this subject in the college. When I tell the story about how tough the class was I always must add that the professor even held class at 6:00 a.m. on the 4th of July. He moved the time to early in the morning so we would still have time with our families or friends the rest of the day. About half the class was there that morning. (By the way, I was one of only 3 people who got an A in the class. One of the other A's was my study partner who was an older student. At the time, she was about my age now.) While I don't remember most of the formulas, one of the things I do remember from the class is how to tell the difference between good research and garbage, or crap. A lot of research many people hear about and report on is garbage! This understanding has proven to be extremely valuable over the years and has helped me find solutions in both my professional and personal life. In the field of health and weight loss we also often hear of research that provides a snippet of information but seems to be unaware of other important information. For example: recently a research study came out saying that it did not matter what time you ate, that all calories are the same, no matter what time consumed. While this is true, it completely omitted or failed to mention that it is more difficult for many to abstain from eating too much when they eat late in the evening. Since then, additional research has reconfirmed the adage to "eat breakfast like a king and... dinner like a popper." We also often see articles written by skinny health fanatics, or people who claim to be, but obviously have no idea what it's like to have been obese and lose a substantial amount of weight and keep it off over a long period of time.

My Old Eating Habits

While I would eat some healthy foods, such as oatmeal in the morning, I would also eat a lot of sugary, fatty, simple carbohydrate foods (crap). All the kinds of foods, that would make me even more sick. I would often find myself trying to eat myself out of depression, lethargy, or fogs. It seemed to work for short periods of time, but never lasted. I loved pastries, ice cream, chips, bread, and many types of candies such as licorice. I loved high fat fried foods such as fried chicken and hamburgers. Not only did I have diabetes and high blood pressure, but fatty liver too. Many of the numbers from my blood work were either too low or too high.

My Low Point

Not only was I morbidly obese, but I would be in terrible pain for days after doing simple things for even short periods of time. I especially remember helping put chairs away after a church event, and on another occasion teaching someone swing dance, something I loved to do despite my morbid obesity. (When I would swing dance, I would usually dance one song, then sit out three or four before I could dance again.) The tightness and pain I would feel after simple activities, coupled with depression and difficulty concentrating were my low point.

> Like most addicts, I was pretty good at rationalizing and thought I was pretty good at hiding. I rationalized that I DID eat a lot of healthy things and I DID walk and get some exercise. Like most addicts though, it was just a lot of rationalization without complete honesty.

What I was eating and how I was caring for my body were also in stark contrast to my values and beliefs.

Eureka

My *eureka* moment came when I discovered some anecdotal information related to Alzheimer's. As mentioned previously, every time I had tried to eat healthier in the past... and eat less... my brain would go into a deep fog. I wondered if something I had read while reading about Alzheimer's might help, and it did. (I'll refer more to the types of meals I now eat in a subsequent chapter. I'm putting this off because, without the habits, skills, and tools, which are my focus here, it wouldn't have been enough.) The anecdotal information I discovered related to a medium chain fatty acid (medium chain triglyceride), virgin organic coconut. Some medium chain oils are easily converted to ketones which can fuel the brain. I only use virgin organic coconut oil.

> If interested you can read <u>Medium Chain Triglyceride Oil Consumption as Part of a Weight Loss Diet Does Not Lead to an Adverse Metabolic Profile When Compared to Olive Oil</u>

It's important to note there is also contradictory information that coconut oil is not good for the body. My personal experience was profound and allowed

http://weight-lossnewsandresearch.blogspot.com/2017/10/medium-chain-triglyceride-oil.html

me to eat less without lower blood sugars and associated brain fog. Some articles I've read advocate as much as 4 tablespoons of coconut oil daily. I use between ½ and 1 tablespoon in one of my smoothies about four to five times per week and that is enough.

I put together a plan based on years of research, wrote my goal in detail, and started my new life. While there were plateaus and some ups and downs, I lost 115 pounds in just over one year and due to the habits, skills, tools, and techniques, have kept it off, within just a few pounds.

For a basic healthy eating plan include:

Fruits (not juice and not too much fruit), **Vegetables** (Be careful to not overeat vegetables, which are high in starch such as corn and potatoes. If you are pregnant or thinking about becoming pregnant, avoid potatoes of all kinds.), **Whole Grains, Legumes, Healthy Fats, Healthy Herbs and Spices, Protein**

Note: Carbohydrates are essential. Eat complex carbohydrates; avoid simple carbohydrates (or similar crap).

http://quickhealthymealsonabudget.blogspot.com/

Food Addictions:

For many, food addictions can be one of the most difficult addictions to overcome. You can quit alcohol, tobacco, illegal drugs, gambling, pornography, etc., but you cannot quit eating or at least consuming calories in any form, without dying. This does not mean any of these addictions are easy to overcome. In most cases, they can be extremely difficult; but all are possible, including a food addiction or binge eating. The long-term consequences of many addictions, even in recovery, can be significantly worse than most food addictions; however, with most addictions, it is possible to overcome the addiction and go on to live a very healthy, happy, productive life. People with food addictions and/or a binge eating disorder must deal intimately with food daily. This makes a food addiction or binge eating disorder unique among addictions.

Though Food Addictions may not be clinically recognized, per se', some people with severe eating problems may have what is classified as a *Feeding and*

This book is designed for the person who just needs to lose a few stubborn pounds and develop a healthier lifestyle, for the "food-addict" or binge eater, and for addicts of any kind.

Eating Disorder, such as *Binge-Eating Disorder* or other similar disorder. Just because someone eats too much, does not mean they have a clinical eating disorder. According to the Diagnostic and Statistical Manual of Mental Disorders, Fifth Edition (DSM-5), "binge-eating disorder is distinct from obesity". I was often a binge eater, especially in times of greater stress and depression. I still can be if I do not maintain, and adjust my recovery plan as needed.

Whether you have a diagnosable eating disorder is not the issue. The bottom line is this… it can be very difficult for some people to control their eating. For many people, this book can help.

Personally, I need a psychological break between times when I can eat and times when I cannot (water is OK.) Much of the time I eat breakfast and I'm done. Because I achieve Food Security at breakfast and include complex carbohydrates, which digest very slowly, I can do this, but it took me about two years to get to this point. For the first year I ate a large breakfast, fairly large lunch, then a very small dinner, snack, or healthy drink. Between the end of the first year and the second year I gradually moved to mostly eating only breakfast. On occasion, I still plan for and will eat lunch, usually for social reason. On even more rare occasions I will plan for and eat dinner, but that tends to cause me to lose control for a few days and I'll over-eat.

If you are a food addict or binge eater you may want to set a plan to never eat after work, or after 5 or 6 at the latest. If your blood sugar is stable and you have sufficient energy and clarity of mind, gradually move that down to not eating after noon or 1. Yes, I am at times hungry in the evening, sometimes very hungry. I've reframed this or come to think of hunger differently than I used to. As long as I have food security, energy, and clarity of mind, and my blood sugar is in good control, hunger represents self-control or power over self. That's a good feeling. This gets easier as you practice and make it a habit, if you have established The Foundation.

> Currently I have made a commitment to the men in one of the addiction recovery groups to not eat in the evening and I have not eaten after 5:02 P.M. since making that commitment, with a few exceptions. Once, while visiting our eldest daughter, I forgot myself and ate. Another time the evening after returning from this visit. During the night, I often have a dry throat which becomes sore and I will suck on a throat lozenge. For a couple of nights my wife had some hard candy and I rationalized it was similar to the lozenges. This was something I would have never eaten during the day when more alert. I realized what I was doing and put a stop to this behavior and my wife has discontinued having it lying around. I also had a couple of lapses in a hotel room on a road trip with my son. Close proximity to your addiction, especially when tired or stressed, is especially difficult.
>
> So, I admit, I've fallen off the wagon on a few occasions. I am solidly back on the wagon now and have been for some time.

> The following is one take or opinion on compulsive eating:
>
> "…compulsive eating is basically a refusal to be fully alive. No matter what we weigh, those of us who are compulsive eaters have anorexia of the soul. We refuse to take in what sustains us. We live lives of

deprivation. And when we can't stand it any longer, we binge. The way we are able to accomplish all of this is by the simple act of bolting -- of leaving ourselves -- hundreds of times a day." — Geneen Roth, Women, Food and God: An Unexpected Path to Almost Everything

Section 2

FIVE HABITS OF WEIGHT LOSS SUCCESS

Some of these may surprise you and you may even want to argue against them; however, I'll provide references and recommend you take the time to read and research if you need convincing. Still not convinced??? Give them an earnest test for a month and see what happens. This is intended to be a Workbook, not just a book to be read and discarded. There will be numerous assignments. Please be prepared to take the time to complete the assignments as you read the book. Please use the space provided to take notes and write your plan and goals. . . In pencil. (If you are reading an electronic version of this book, please keep a notebook on hand, take notes, and write your plan, goals, and objectives.)

> "Habits, scientists say, emerge because the brain is constantly looking for ways to save effort. Left to its own devices, the brain will try to make almost any routine into a habit, because habits allow our minds to ramp down more often. This effort-saving instinct is a huge advantage. An efficient brain requires less room... An efficient brain also allows us to stop thinking constantly about basic behaviors, such as walking and choosing what to eat..." - _The Power of Habit: Why we do what we do in life and business_. Charles Duhigg pgs. 17 & 19

HABIT # 1

WEIGH YOURSELF EVERY-DAY AT THE SAME TIME AND RECORD YOUR WEIGHT

(Do it in the same clothes, i.e. your underwear, and without shoes.)

I know, I jumped right into a controversial topic. You've probably heard that it's too discouraging to weigh every day and you should never weigh more than once a week. After I had lost 30 or 50 pounds, I heard many people still struggling to lose weight tell me how wrong I was... How ironic!

Fact: Most people who lose a significant amount of weight and keep it off, weigh themselves daily.

> Easy to read article:
>
> http://weight-lossnewsandresearch.blogspot.com/2013/10/daily-self-weighing-helps-study.html
>
> More research:
>
> http://weight-lossnewsandresearch.blogspot.com/2017/09/weight-loss-and-daily-weighing.html
>
> Research Abstracts:
>
> *Self-Monitoring in Weight Loss: A Systematic Review of the Literature*
>
> http://www.sciencedirect.com/science/article/pii/S0002822310016445
>
> *Self-weighing in weight gain prevention and weight loss trials*
>
> http://link.springer.com/article/10.1207/s15324796abm3003_5

Why is daily weighing important?

Daily data is important for almost any significant transformation. It provides you with frequent feedback and can help you review what you may have done to lose, gain, or stay the same. This habit

> Note: For almost all the research articles listed, you will be able to read the abstract free of charge but will need to purchase the article from the journal publisher or go to a good library that carries scientific journals if you wish to read the entire article. These articles are just a small sampling of the research that is available on the various subjects. If you have difficulty linking to the article, you can also do an online search for the title of the article.

alone will help some people lose weight for a short period of time; however, by itself, it's not enough for long term success. While *The Foundation*, Habits, Tools, Skills, and Techniques, are fundamental for almost everyone, everyone also has different needs and situations. Collecting data daily will help you better understand your individual needs and help you discover and better understand what works for you and what does not. You will learn more about your personal deadly or difficult cues and "gateway foods." As you record your data pertaining to what you weigh and other data listed in subsequent chapters of this book, also record how you feel and your energy level. You can do this with a simple system of rating how you feel from 0-5, your energy level from 0-5, and your mind/thought clarity from 0-5. I know there are some of you thinking: "I don't have time for this." My question in response: Do you have time to struggle feeling like crap, without being able to think clearly? Do you have the time and money to be sick and/or in pain? If none of these are issues for you, perhaps this book isn't for you. Because all of this has become habit and I use an online tool to record my data, it has become quick and easy. It may take time, but it can become quick and easy for you too.

Over the past few years, I have rarely needed to take time off from work because of illness. While I have taken sick time, it has almost always been to help my wife through surgeries.

Warning:

Some weight fluctuations may seem to not make sense. They are often due to your retention or loss of water. This can be caused by how much sodium (salt) you consume and even, to a lesser extent by the amount of carbohydrates you consume. Remember, the right amount of sodium, water, and complex carbohydrates are essential for a healthy diet and a healthy you. As you incorporate this habit into your life, you will most likely begin to recognize the reasons for and expect the fluctuations. For example: While I rarely drink soda, I came to realize that when I did drink a diet soda, it would cause an upwards weight fluctuation due mostly to additional water retention. By the way, diet soda more often correlates with weight gain than weight loss. Diet soda still falls under the crap column, but may not be quite as "crappy" as regular. I am currently working on eliminating it from my diet.

I cannot tell you what the right amount of sodium or water is for you. It varies by individual, from individual to individual and is also related to health conditions.

Consult with your physician and/or dietitian about what the "right amount" is for you.

Tip:
As mentioned above, I use a free online calculator to record my daily weight. You can do a simple search for free online calorie counters or go here to find a link to a list.
http://weight-lossnewsandresearch.blogspot.com/2017/08/free-online-calorie-counters.html
You'll want to use one that allows you to record consumption, weight, and exercise. Most of the people in my classes have used either loseit or Myfitnesspal. You can find a link to those on the page above as well.

HABIT # 2
EAT OR DRINK A HEALTHY BREAKFAST EVERY DAY
AND
RECORD ALL CALORIC INTAKE

For many years, this has been somewhat of a given. It has been considered general knowledge that breakfast is the most important meal of the day. Some recent research has made this a little more controversial or even confusing. This controversy isn't necessarily because the research was bad, but because as often occurs, the reporting of the research was at times a bit shallow, limited, or shortsighted. Sometimes researchers are not aware of conflicting or confounding information or variables. Sometimes research is poorly conducted or executed.

As mentioned earlier in this book, reports of a recent study claimed it did not make any difference what time of day you ate or drank your calories but only the number of calories. Technically, this is true; however, it misses two incredibly important pieces of the puzzle, stress and fatigue.

Some of you may have seen the comical "stress diet." There are different versions, but it usually starts with the person eating something like half a grapefruit for breakfast. For lunch, they may have a salad and one cookie. For a mid-afternoon snack, they eat the rest of the package of cookies. For dinner, they have a plate of pasta and a small bowl of ice-cream and at bedtime they eat the rest of the ice-cream.

This is intended to be a humorous but all too familiar joke; however, there is basic science behind this humor. Our brain is sometimes categorized as "old brain" and "new brain." Science often associates, our "new brain" with: cognition, thoughts, and planning (reflective). The "old brain" is often associated with: habits, impulse (reactive or reflexive), and automatic (life essential) functions (such as breathing) and emotions. Our old brain regulates most of the critical functions we need to stay alive and protect us from imminent physical danger (fight, flight, or freeze response). When we become tired or stressed, our old brain tends to have more influence on our behavior and our new brain tends to lose influence. This is one of the reasons "positive well-developed habits" and prior planning, are so especially critical when we are stressed and/or tired. Often it is not enough to have decided what you will do in a critical situation. Often you must also practice that response, make it a habit, and prearranged your environment. You can also purposely reprogram yourself to respond to difficult cues with a healthy and helpful response. In sports, great athletes and in the arts, great artists practice responding to cues in desired and productive ways. We can learn to do the same by making small, deliberate, changes, over time, and practicing those changes.

As we go through our day and become more stressed and tired, our thoughtful, practical reflective self may have less control over our behavior, less ability to think through problems rationally. We become more reactive. The tools and skills we'll discuss later can help. Changing our habits and developing new positive behaviors and responses (habits) can help---a lot! There are foods which used to be very tempting and almost impossible for me to resist when tired or stressed. Because of newly ingrained habits, I can now easily resist most of these foods even when stressed or tired. I can even resist them when others around me are eating them. They have lost their power over me. . . So to speak. However; there are still some foods I have a harder time resisting when tired or stressed.

Alcohol, stress, fatigue, marijuana, and many both legal and illegal drugs decrease the influence of the new brain and increase the influence of the old. Decrease or eliminate these to the extent possible and you will increase your positive self-control. When we are stressed or tired or under the influence of alcohol or many drugs we tend to react instead of act. We become more reactive and less reflexive or thoughtful. We tend to forfeit self-control and our best thinking. Our behavior tends to default to impulse and habit.

We can change our reaction and increase our positive self-control through new habits and training ourselves to respond in more positive, productive ways to the powerful cues in our environment. However; this requires willful, planful, purposeful practice.

> Here's a little more information on the relation between the "old brain" and habits.
>
> First an easier to read article:
>
> Habits: *How They Form And How To Break Them* (or how to change them)
>
> http://responsiblepracticalparenting.blogspot.com/2014/12/habits-how-they-form-and-how-to-break.html
>
> And more research:
>
> *A Critical Review of Habit Learning and the Basal Ganglia*
>
> http://weight-lossnewsandresearch.blogspot.com/2017/12/a-critical-review-of-habit-learning-and.html
>
> *The role of the basal ganglia in habit formation*
>
> http://weight-lossnewsandresearch.blogspot.com/2017/12/the-role-of-basal-ganglia-in-habit.html
>
> More research
>
> http://weight-lossnewsandresearch.blogspot.com/2017/09/basal-ganglia-and-habits.html

Remember, it's not practice that makes perfect, it is perfect practice that makes perfect.

Fact:

Most people who lose a substantial amount of weight and keep it off eat and/or drink a healthy breakfast every morning.

> Easy to read article:

You may have heard the old saying, "Eat breakfast like a king, lunch like a queen, and dinner like a pauper." There is some recent research which indicates for Type 2 Diabetics, two large meals (remember *The Foundation*) a day may be better than many smaller meals. There are also some studies indicating that multiple smaller meals, throw off insulin and grehlin (helps to regulate hunger). Most days I eat a robust and very healthy breakfast, and **if** I eat lunch it is a smaller but equally healthy lunch. I try not to eat again the rest of the day. This is part of "my plan." This is also a form of intermittent fasting; which research indicates is helpful for our health and memory. This research indicates intermittent fasting may help keep your brain healthier, longer, a good thing for people such as myself who are concerned about Alzheimer's. The Foundation can also help memory. This strategy works for me and is something I do, but may not be necessary or practical for you. If you are diabetic and try something like this, you will want to keep an even closer than usual watch on your blood sugar levels to make sure you remain safe. Before trying anything like this, consult with your physician and follow his or her advice. I eat complex carbohydrates, such as rolled oats, rolled barley, and brown rice, which are digested very slowly in the body. I almost always consume healthy protein with the complex carbohydrates.

> http://weight-lossnewsandresearch.blogspot.com/2013/07/5-quick-and-easy-breakfast-recipes-for.html
>
> Research:
>
> *Long-Term Weight Loss and Breakfast in Subjects in the National Weight Control Registry*
>
> http://weight-lossnewsandresearch.blogspot.com/2015/01/long-term-weight-loss-and-breakfast-in.html
>
> *Who succeeds in maintaining weight loss? A conceptual review of factors associated with weight loss maintenance and weight regain*
>
> http://weight-lossnewsandresearch.blogspot.com/2017/12/who-succeeds-in-maintaining-weight-loss.html
>
> More research
>
> http://weight-lossnewsandresearch.blogspot.com/2017/09/breakfast-and-weight-loss.html

From time to time I eat only a very large breakfast and have great energy and can think clearly all day. Fasting from breakfast to breakfast is also a technique I use when I need to regain self-control.

> Two easy to read articles:
>
> http://weight-lossnewsandresearch.blogspot.com/2014/05/2-large-meals-good-for-diabetics-health.html
>
> http://weight-lossnewsandresearch.blogspot.com/2014/05/sun-news-two-large-meals-may-be-better.html

One of the reasons I usually don't eat dinner is because I have trouble "eating just one" of almost anything, especially when tired or stressed. Some of you may remember the old commercial where the person says something like: "betcha can't eat just one?" Well, when I'm tired or stressed, that's me for almost anything! During those more difficult times of greater temptation it's easier for me to say "No" or "No thank you" than to have "just one" of almost anything I find even remotely tasty. (Sometimes even things I DON'T find tasty.)

> **More related information and research.**
>
> Basal Ganglia and Habits:
>
> http://weight-lossnewsandresearch.blogspot.com/2017/08/basal-ganglia-and-habits.html
>
> The importance of breakfast for weight loss:
>
> http://weight-lossnewsandresearch.blogspot.com/2017/08/the-importance-of-breakfast-for-weight.html
>
> You will find some conflicting information.

Most of the research referenced previously in this book and pertaining to intermittent fasting is different from the way I do this. As I was starting to lose weight, I ate three to four meals a day. As I lost weight and learned to eat

> More research:
>
> *The effect of feeding frequency on insulin and ghrelin responses in human subjects*
>
> http://weight-lossnewsandresearch.blogspot.com/2017/12/the-effect-of-feeding-frequency-on.html
>
> *Intermittent fasting dissociates beneficial effects of dietary restriction on glucose metabolism and neuronal resistance to injury from calorie intake*
>
> http://weight-lossnewsandresearch.blogspot.com/2017/12/intermittent-fasting-dissociates.html
>
> *Beneficial effects of intermittent fasting and caloric restriction on the cardiovascular and cerebrovascular systems*
>
> http://weight-lossnewsandresearch.blogspot.com/2017/12/beneficial-effects-of-intermittent.html
>
> *Apparent Prolongation of the Life Span of Rats by Intermittent Fasting: One Figure*
>
> http://weight-lossnewsandresearch.blogspot.com/2018/01/apparent-prolongation-of-life-span-of.html
>
> *Caloric restriction and intermittent fasting: Two potential diets for successful brain aging*
>
> http://weight-lossnewsandresearch.blogspot.com/2018/01/caloric-restriction-and-intermittent.html
>
> *Final Answer: Ghrelin Can Suppress Insulin Secretion in Humans, but Is It Clinically Relevant?*
>
> http://weight-lossnewsandresearch.blogspot.com/2018/01/final-answer-ghrelin-can-suppress.html

healthier, I dropped that to only one or two meals a day while eating only one large breakfast most of the time.

I can do this because I establish Food Security at breakfast and this includes complex carbohydrates and protein.

You have probably heard or read, and this is true, you should always take a pre-written list when you shop for groceries.

> More research
>
> http://weight-lossnewsandresearch.blogspot.com/2017/09/2-meals-day-for-t2-diabetics.html
>
> http://weight-lossnewsandresearch.blogspot.com/2017/09/intermittent-fasting-benefits.html
>
> While not yet conclusive, there is some research intermittent fasting may also be beneficial for people with type 2 diabetes. If you try this, you need to work especially close with your physician and measure your blood sugar as often as recommended.
>
> http://weight-lossnewsandresearch.blogspot.com/2017/10/intermittent-fasting-and-diabetes.html
>
> http://weight-lossnewsandresearch.blogspot.com/2017/10/intermittent-fasting-and-weight-loss.html

This decreases the chance of impulse buying and unhealthy purchases. I will add another recommendation. Never shop for groceries when you are tired, hungry, or stressed. This will also help you make healthier decisions and reduce or eliminate impulse buying. I am not perfect and still mess up from time to time and must remember and recommit to my plan. A couple of years ago I needed just a few things from the grocery store. It was later in the evening (poor planning). While I was getting the items on my list, I had the thought that a package of sugar free ice-cream bars would be nice. I found and bought them. While driving home in the car, I had the thought that I "could eat just one." By the time I went to bed the entire package had been eaten, by me. Remember, when it comes to food or snacks, sugar free usually doesn't mean calorie free and quite often there are unhealthy additives.

This brings me to another very important point that I'll talk about again and again, learn to "fail forward." We all make mistakes. When you do, you may feel like you deserve an "F" and should just give up; but F also stands for feedback. Use that feedback to adjust your plan and move forward.

So, what is a healthy breakfast?

First, what it is not. It is not pastries and it is not sugary cold cereal. It could be: eggs and whole wheat toast, cooked old fashioned rolled oats, one piece or a small bowl of fruit and a no sugar yogurt. Or perhaps my own personal favorite, a very healthy smoothie that creates food security.

A breakfast shake or smoothie is the foundation of my daily eating plan. My breakfast shake or smoothie is HUGE according to many of my friends. There is an adage in the restaurant business that the two cheapest ingredients you can add to any food are water and air. Well, it just so happens that those two ingredients also have the fewest calories. . . Right at zero. Eating, or in my case drinking, a huge healthy breakfast is both physically and psychologically filling. The added water and air (due to the foam) makes it appear even more filling. I can still eat a couple pieces of whole wheat toast with the smoothie. That gives me something to chew with the smoothie. This is not the only thing I have for breakfast. I rotate and eat other meals, but a smoothie is what I most often drink.

Complex carbohydrates and protein are essential for breakfast. The Foundation and meeting Food Security are best.

One more note:

You may have also heard the term "mindless eating". It's something I was in the habit of doing, right along with "grazing." It's something many do without realizing how much they eat and drink. For most of you, when you start recording ALL your caloric intake, you will be shocked. I used to have a very overweight friend who would joke that he would eat the leftover crumbs because all the calories had fallen out. Obviously, that is not true and it can be amazing how much you eat when you graze, or just "pick at food/drinks" throughout the day. Recording your entire caloric intake every day will help you both better control what you eat and understand where you need to make changes. Recording caloric intake in advance is even better. Planning, writing out that plan, and then practicing following that plan, are all helpful strategies for any addiction recovery.

I have not been perfect at this; however, over the past seven years I have recorded about 95 to 97% of everything I have eaten and everything caloric I have drunk. I'm still not at 100%.

For some people, recording everything they eat or drink every day and the associated calories is enough to help them lose weight. But, there is much more you can do to get even better results and make it last!

Both loseit.com and myfitnesspal.com will help you set a budget. Your budget will change as you lose weight. Never go below 1200 calories or 33 grams of fat per day. Both minimal calories and healthy fats are essential for health.

Old fashioned rolled oats are a great way to start your day. They can be easily used in smoothies, as I often do. (Rolled barley can also be a great addition for a morning smoothie.) Rolled oats can also be prepared in many other easy ways. You can add them to yogurt and add other items such as raisins, nuts, and other fruits. You can put about ½ cup of rolled oats in a bowl and pour in water until the water is about ½ inch above the oats, then place in the microwave for about 1 minute. You can cook in a pan of water; bring it to a boil, then add honey, cinnamon, and raisins or other fruit.

This can be a great start towards food security and provide great complex carbohydrates, which can help

> One more research resource:
>
> http://weight-lossnewsandresearch.blogspot.com/2017/12/breakfast-and-diabetes.html

provide satiation for a long time during your day. When I purchase old fashioned rolled oats, I buy in the large 25 lb., bags, which makes them especially inexpensive.

HABIT # 3
EXERCISE EVERY DAY
AND
RECORD YOUR EXERCISE

I use the same free online calorie counter to record my exercise. It provides good feedback on how many calories I can eat and remain within my budget. I sometimes find I need to eat a few hundred fewer calories than the counter tells me. That's OK; I've just learned to adjust. This is another testament to the importance of data and adjusting according to personal needs. This is quite common for people who have lost a great deal of weight, as I have, and who continue to maintain that weight loss. Our metabolisms seem to adjust and need fewer calories for maintenance. This is another reason Food Security, is so essential. You can easily reach Food Security daily, and remain within your personal calorie and fat budget. Exercise allows you to increase your budget, according to the amount and type of exercise and your own personal situation as learned through personal data.

There are a few people out there, perhaps 10 - 15% who can and will, by themselves, go out of their way to a gym every day or multiple times a week and be able to sustain this effort year after year. I am not one of them. Gyms and athletic clubs make a great deal of money from people who make New Year's Resolutions, purchase a membership for the year and then over the first few months gradually reduce their attendance to rarely or never.

For most of us, there are two things that will substantially increase the chance we will maintain an exercise program:

1. Make exercise a part of your natural routine within your natural environment.
2. Exercise with a friend or other support.

Fact: People are more likely to maintain an exercise program if they make it a part of their natural routine and within their natural environment.

Fact: People are more likely to maintain an exercise program if they do it with a friend, or at least have the ongoing support of a friend. This can include a pet such as a dog who wants and needs to exercise and will remind you it's time to go.

Why?

There are natural cues all around us, all the time. These "cues" are reminders. . . Or sometimes overwhelming enticers or persuaders to get you to do or not to do something. Cues can be either positive or negative. When your alarm goes off in the morning, it is a cue or reminder that it is time to get up. The sound of a rooster, the light from the morning sun, or the call from a parent, may also be cues that it's time to get up. We have cues throughout the day and night, natural cues that tell us it's time to eat, time to drink, or time to use the bathroom. These cues can be extremely powerful. However, we can create new cues which are just as or almost as powerful. New cues that tell us it's time to exercise and even cues that remind us about better nutritional choices or why losing or maintaining a healthy weight is important.

When you begin to use the natural environment for exercise, you can use those natural cues to help remind you to exercise. It becomes habit and your "old brain" pushes you to continue this habit in response to the cues in your natural environment and routine. Some people put their walking shoes on a chair in the room where they may sit to watch TV or relax after work to remind them they need to exercise before sitting down. Some people may put signs or notes or other cues to make the important behavioral choices or remind them these changes are personally important. Some people may put pictures of their grandchildren next to exercise equipment in the house to remind them they want to be around to see those grandchildren grow up. Some people may want to put that exercise equipment someplace where they almost trip over it in the living room, instead of in a room they seldom visit, to remind them to exercise.

I keep stretch tubes on my credenza at work. When I arrive, I move them to my desk. This reminds me of a series of exercises I do every day in my office. The last of these exercises uses those stretch tubes and when I'm done I put them back on my credenza.

If you have and walk a dog, you might keep the leash on or next to your front door to remind you to take your dog for a walk. If this becomes a habit, your dog may also start to remind you. My dog Belle often reminds me that I need to take her for a good long walk. Cues are powerful reminders and motivators for both good and bad. You can use those cues and create new ones to help you make better choices. There will be a more about cues in the last chapter of this book.

Friends, family members, and other social supports can also be powerful cues to help us maintain an exercise program. If you meet someone in the neighborhood for a walk in the morning, afternoon, or early evening, you can create mutual support and even a little positive guilt to help you maintain the habit. (Yes, even <u>a little guilt</u> can be a positive influence at times.)

One of the mistakes many people make in starting an exercise program is trying to do too much too quickly. Don't try for a complete turnaround in what you are doing today. Start with slight changes and PLAN for long-term and substantial transformations. Create a firm foundation of a healthy, well-balanced diet, moderate to light exercise, stress management and sleep hygiene, then slowly build upon that foundation.

> Research:
>
> *Evaluation and modification of exercise patterns in the natural environment.*
>
> http://weight-lossnewsandresearch.blogspot.com/2018/01/evaluation-and-modification-of-exercise.html
>
> *Predictors of exercise participation in female hospital nurses.*
>
> http://weight-lossnewsandresearch.blogspot.com/2018/01/predictors-of-exercise-participation-in.html
>
> *Social-Cognitive Predictors of Physical Exercise Adherence: Three Longitudinal Studies in Rehabilitation*
>
> http://weight-lossnewsandresearch.blogspot.com/2018/01/social-cognitive-predictors-of-physical.html
>
> *Predictors of adoption and maintenance of vigorous physical activity in men and women*
>
> http://weight-lossnewsandresearch.blogspot.com/2018/01/predictors-of-adoption-and-maintenance.html

> "Don't try to overhaul your life overnight. Instead, focus on making one small change at a time. Over time those small changes will add up to a big transformation. Don't give up."   Author unknown

Always consult with your doctor or other medical practitioner before starting an exercise program. Starting an exercise program and hurting yourself is setting yourself up for failure and is almost like sabotaging your own efforts. Make small changes; listen to good medical advice from your medical practitioner, someone who knows you. Some people may also want to consult with a physical therapist. **The most important aspect of exercise is safety.** Stretch before exercising and when doing strength or resistance exercise, icing for about 15 minutes afterwards can be useful for some.

When I first started to exercise in earnest again, I couldn't do a single pushup without days of pain in my neck and shoulders. I would do one pushup, then ice for about 15 minutes. I did that for about a week, then went to two pushups for about a week, then 4, then six etc. I have done the same thing with almost every exercise I do. Now every weekday when I get to work, the exercise tubes remind me of a few brief exercises I do every day in my office. They are cues in my natural environment that now almost compel me to do these exercises every day I'm at work. They take only about 8 minutes per day, but make a huge difference. While they take a little time out of my day, I count this as my break time and they also make me more productive. I feel better physically and mentally.

On the weekends, I usually go for a longer walk with Belle. On weekdays, I walk to and from work and take Belle for short walk most days. Not everyone can do that, but most people can park their car a little further from work so they can walk, or get off the bus or subway one or two stations further from their work. You may also want to park a little further out in the store parking lot, take the stairs, and walk to talk briefly with a co-worker in another office instead of calling or sending an email (also helps build relationships). During weekdays, I usually walk 3-4 miles a day, plus the exercises mentioned above. You do not need to exercise as much as I do. It just allows me to eat more, so I exercise more.

There is even a term for one type of exercising in your home called "Couchersizing." You'll find links to exercises and videos on the same webpage.

> Here are some additional ideas with videos of exercises you might be able to do in your home or work place:
>
> http://weight-lossnewsandresearch.blogspot.com/2017/08/exercises-for-home-or-office.html

The key here is to look for, find ways to, and do even small things at first which over time will amount to a greater transformation. Milton Erickson, a famous American psychiatrist, believed that as humans, most of us get into some sort of rut. He believed that over time, huge positive changes can occur by just getting people out of their rut, with just a slight change in the right direction. For a pilot, just a one-degree variance off course can, over time, make the difference between safely reaching the desired destination or ending up in disaster. Starting with a slight positive change for you, can make a substantial difference over time.

Do not fall into the false trap that you don't have enough time to exercise. Exercising, but not to excess, over time, provides you with more time to be productive, not less. If you eat healthy and exercise, most people will have much less sick time and live a longer more productive life. If you learn to manage your stress positively, you will prolong your life and expand your productivity even more. If you incorporate exercise into your natural routine in your natural environment, it will become second nature, a new habit.

I recently saw a great cartoon with a doctor asking his patient: "What fits your busy schedule better, exercising one hour a day or being dead 24 hours a day?" http://www.glasbergen.com/ This book is not going to insist you exercise an hour a day, though it is an interesting question.

If you are someone who likes to go to the gym or wants to go to the gym, but has had difficulty maintaining this over time, there are a few things you can do to increase the chance you will maintain. Find a friend or support group who will go with you and encourage you to continue the effort. If you are a gym owner, help your patrons organize support groups to develop friendships and keep each other motivated and coming to the gym. There will always be that group of people who will do it on their own, but if you want the experience to last for your patrons and want to grow your business, make it not only a positive physical experience but a positive social experience for everyone who might need the additional support.

Some people may exercise in different ways, at different times, and in different places. Some people may cross-train, and that's great. For many starting out, the more consistent it is, the easier it will be to make it a habit. As much as possible, exercise at the same time, in **basically** the same way with some variation, and in the same place, every day. . . Or most days. I have the same basic routine on work days and a different routine on the weekends. It is helpful to mix it up a little. Try different hikes or walks on occasion. Try a different strength/resistance exercise on occasion, but the consistency will help make it a habit which you feel more compelled to continue. This will especially be true if you exercise with natural supports such as your children, grandchildren, spouse, friends, neighbors, colleagues, or even a pet. You will increase your chance of success by purposely placing cues/reminders in your environment to keep you moving.

If there are cues that entice you to not exercise, if possible, remove them or put them someplace out of sight. For example, if your intent is to exercise as soon as you return home in the evening and a huge television and comfortable chair is loudly calling your name, you may have to make a choice between health, and the television and chair. If you have the money and are so inclined, there is exercise equipment you can set up so that the TV only operates when the exercise equipment is being used. Two of the ways to do this is to use exercise equipment that generates electricity or simply turns the TV on or off. If the TV is still too enticing, and you're not able to consistently choose exercise first, you may have to choose between the TV and health.

If, on the other hand, you exercise in the morning, problem solved. You won't have to worry about it when you get home and if you want, you can just sit down and relax.

HABIT # 4
SHARE WHAT YOU LEARN
HELP OTHERS
AND FIND OR CREATE A SYSTEM OF SUPPORT

Fact: Most people who lose a large amount of weight and keep it off have a support and accountability system where they both receive support from and provide support to others, AND where there is appropriate, loving, and meaningful accountability.

Truth be told, there may be people in your life that would *rather* you not change. They may not be willing to admit it to you; they may not even be willing to admit it to themselves. They may be quite comfortable in their own "rut" and if you get out of yours, they might fear they will have to get out of theirs. **('Misery loves company.')** There are lots of social and psychological reasons why any of us may resist or discourage healthy change. We won't go into all the thousands of possible reasons why someone may not want to change or may not want you to change. We'll just leave this topic with a quote from **Milton Erickson, "Change will lead to insight far more often than insight will lead to change."**

Walter Gong was an educator and proponent of the idea that teachers must be learners and learners must be teachers. The best way we incorporate an idea into our own lives is by learning and sharing that idea with others. As you learn and incorporate these habits, skills, and tools, into your own life and turn around and help others do the same, these habits will become a part of you. They can eventually become more powerful than some of the destructive habits you may have now. When someone teaches someone else, they usually hold themselves to a higher standard in what they are teaching. (Not always, but usually.) Most people understand they need to be an example of what they teach.

I'm a big Star Trek fan and love the line spoken by Spock in *Star Trek IV, The Undiscovered Planet*, "Nature abhors a vacuum." This is a basic behavioral concept. If you want to get rid of a bad habit, you need to replace it with a more desirable habit and preferably one that provides for the same underlying need as the old habit. Quite often the underlying need is very different from what you might think. There are always healthier alternatives to any negative or inappropriate urge or need. As stated previously, I also love the book: *Love is Letting Go of Fear* by Gerald Jampolsky which talks about replacing fear with love. Part of your replacement behavior can be helping and lifting others. If you participate in a Diabetes Prevention Program, you may want to become a volunteer lifestyle coach and help others. If you are involved with a 12 Step Program such as Alcoholics Anonymous, or a program like TOPS, you may want to become a facilitator or mentor after you are in recovery and "standing on higher ground." There can be benefit, for both you and others.

Later in this book you'll learn some important concepts around *Incompatible Behaviors* and *Alternative Behaviors* which can help you replace less healthy with healthier habits. Hopefully they will provide for some of the same underlying needs through new and better habits.

So, what kind of support system do you need? You need, we all need, a support system that will hold us accountable without demeaning, and help us replace unhealthy behaviors with better or best behaviors.

Who are the people in your life who might do this for you? Who are the people in your life who may be willing to take this journey with you? Who are those you may be able to help as you learn and incorporate these habits, skills, and tools, into your own life? Doing this will make the difference between just reading a book and changing your life and helping others change theirs, for the better **if,** they are willing, interested, and able.

Please make a list of people who may support you here:

Please make a list of people who you may be able to help (provide resources or information) here: (Some of these people may the same as those in the previous list.) You may simply invite them to join you in a local support or recovery group.

When I set my initial goal of losing 100 pounds, I announced it to everyone I knew on Facebook, everyone at work, and all my other friends and family. I then posted regular updates on my progress and even some of my struggles. I did this because I understood and wanted to enlist the power of social pressure and social support. After I had lost about 70 pounds, and according to my body mass index was still obese, I had a lot of people telling me, 'that's enough.' I was starting to get some social pressure to stop losing weight. Fortunately, I was determined and still had the positive support of a few. By then, the habits were fairly, though not perfectly internalized and had become an integral part of who I now am. New habits had replaced many old habits and the benefits of feeling better both physically and mentally had become powerful motivators in my life. I had also developed the self-efficacy to keep going despite obstacles, and despite the opinion of some who had previously been supportive.

Once I had lost 100 pounds I realized I was only 13 pounds from being within the "normal range" according to body mass index, and so I reset my goal and lost another 15 pounds.

Yes, you can use, just as I did, the internet for social support. There is even some research that indicates there may be a positive benefit when it is done anonymously. However; to be held accountable, in a loving and supportive manner, or to help hold others accountable in a loving and supportive manner, it is much more difficult when anonymous.

> Research:
>
> *Benefits of recruiting participants with friends and increasing social support for weight loss and maintenance.*
>
> http://weight-lossnewsandresearch.blogspot.com/2018/01/benefits-of-recruiting-participants.html
>
> *Social support in an Internet weight loss community*
>
> http://weight-lossnewsandresearch.blogspot.com/2018/01/social-support-in-internet-weight-loss.html

While you may include paid professionals in your support team, most cannot afford this luxury. As much as possible you will want to enlist natural supports, people you connect with on a daily or weekly basis for support. If they are the type of people who will encourage and provide genuine help, you will want to enlist the support of friends, family members, and even colleagues at work. When possible, do this as a team effort in the home and/or work. If others in these important environments are working for the same goal, or even supporting you in yours, they may be willing to change some of those challenging cues (temptations). For example, ask them to remove the pastries from the table in the break room or the counter next to you, or move them further from your work station, or out of your frequent walking path. You, may also want to replace those temptations with something healthier.

While I highly encourage you to enlist and develop your own support system, you can also use a Facebook page I have created and where I periodically add news and research regarding weight loss and other health issues. It is located here:
https://www.facebook.com/DeliciousNutritionStealthHealth/. This page can help you connect with others with whom you can provide mutual support.

Your support system will be most effective, as you develop collaborative, mutually supportive relationships. Unfortunately, many have lost sight of their own capacity. Many have lost the belief they can accomplish even the simplest of goals. They have partially lost the requisite self-efficacy (belief in their own abilities) to solve problems and expand capacity. In *Psycho-Cybernetics*, Maxwell Maltz wrote: **"Often the only difference between a success and a failure is not one's better abilities or ideas, but the courage (and I believe self-efficacy) that one has to bet on *one's* ideas, to take a calculated risk - -and to act."**

Even if there are people in your life who seem to sabotage your positive efforts to be healthier, establish a circle of support that will help propel you forward and upward.

> "If you accept the expectations of others, especially negative ones, then you never will change the outcome." Michael Jordan

In relation to an addiction there are two types of people out there, friends and accomplices. Friends help and support you in overcoming your addiction. They encourage you and purposely help you avoid cues that might encourage you to indulge in your addiction. If you are an alcoholic, a friend would not drink around you and would not take you places where alcohol is being served. If you have a gambling addiction, a friend would not take you to a casino. If you have a food addiction, they would not tempt you with crap. An accomplice does the opposite, sometimes because they don't want you to change, don't really care, don't understand, or sometimes because "misery loves company." If you have accomplices in your life, talk with them about your desire to change and ask them to help. Tell them how they can help by keeping personally unhealthy cues far from you. Let them know what those cues are. They may be totally unaware of some sights, sounds, or smells that cause your cravings. If they are not willing to help, you may need to find better friends. An accomplice is someone who tempts you, belittles you in your efforts to change, or asks you to accompany them, or even just "drop them off" where your addiction flourishes.

One great opportunity for support may be the Diabetes Prevention Program. You can find links to information about the program as well as where to find it. The Diabetes Prevention Program will provide great science based information, a coach, and pears to help you make needed changes and progress. Once you have made the changes you want and need, you may want to turn around and become a coach yourself. As a group participant, you can help others. As a coach, you can help others make dramatic healthy changes in their lives. I have had the great satisfaction of seeing remarkable weight loss, and health improvement for both men and women in my classes.

There is power in commitment. There is great power in covenants. A covenant is an agreement with a promise. It requires another party or person with whom you make this agreement and promise. You must report to this person on at least a weekly basis. This person must in-turn be willing and able to hold you accountable in a loving and supportive, carefrontational manner if needed. If you are an addict of any kind, or binge eater, this must be a part of your life long plan. This person may need to change over time, but this is essential to lifelong success. Mentors and support groups are extremely important for almost any addiction. Get a mentor and find an appropriate support group. When you are able, be a mentor, or facilitate, or co-facilitate a support group.

http://weight-lossnewsandresearch.blogspot.com/2017/08/diabetes-preventon-program.html

I have been a diabetes prevention lifestyle coach for many years and recently started another class. My wife and I are also facilitators for two addiction recovery groups. We have been doing this for a couple of years. I have grown to love and respect many people who attend this program. Many have been through the program previously. They talk about and encourage the changes they are seeing in each other. I have seen remarkable changes and growth. Though I volunteer for both the diabetes prevention program and a 12 Step Program, I honestly get more from these programs than I give. I have spoken with the men in the larger group about my own food addiction and binge eating disorder. I have made a commitment to them to not eat in the evening or at night. Since making that commitment I have *rarely* eaten anything after 5:00 P.M... One evening not so long ago after a very stressful day and week, at about 6: P.M., I took a bite out of an apple and immediately thought of them and my commitment to them. I spit the piece of the apple out of my mouth and put the rest in the refrigerator and ate it in the morning. (I mentioned a couple of my relapses earlier in the book. I am now soundly back on track.)

I know, one apple may not sound like a big deal, negligible fat and few calories. The problem is as a binge eater, it would have started me eating more, but most importantly, I had made a commitment to those men. That commitment to them, has kept me from eating late at night many times. These men are working hard to make substantial changes in their lives. I know I will be reporting to them and if I did not keep my commitment, how could I expect them to keep theirs?

Not too long ago I was on a business trip in another time zone and someone asked me about going to dinner. I explained my commitment and the response was that in the time zone where I resided, it wasn't after 5: P.M. I responded that would be a rationalization and I would not want them to rationalize and I would not either. I did it in a nice way and this person understood and was supportive.

Everyone in recovery of any kind needs a mentor. Some programs call this person a sponsor. If you are an addict, connect with a program and ask for a mentor or sponsor. This person may change over time, but s/he is important and can play a significant role in both your recovery and maintenance. This is not meant to relinquish you of any personal responsibility, but to provide assistance, support, and at times, carefrontation, or loving, stern feedback. When you are strong enough, consider being a mentor yourself.

> "One thing that every great leader, athlete, and talented person has that helps make them the best at what they do is a coach. They all have help. Can you imagine Pau Gasol or Serena Williams without a coach? How about Floyd Mayweather? Of course not! Why would we think that these greats need help but we can do it by ourselves?
>
> A product of my deepest learnings over the past few years as a coach, boils down to a simple sentence, and it's this "We all need help and it's okay!"
>
> When I started in the coaching field 30 years ago, no CEO would admit to having a coach. They would have been ashamed to have a coach. Today this has changed. One thing that I'm very proud of is that in my book Triggers 27 major CEOs endorsed the book. They proudly admit to getting help.
>
> To me, this is much healthier. We've all got behaviors we've been working on for decades. Say we want to be a better listener. We vow to change and yet we don't. Why is making this promise to ourselves again today going to make us different tomorrow? It's not. We have to admit we need help and it's okay! Admitting we need help makes a significant positive difference for all of us.
>
> In my own life, I pay a woman to call me on the phone every day. Why? My name is Marshall Goldsmith. I'm the world's leading executive coach. I was ranked number one leadership thinker in the world. I pay a woman to call me on the phone every day. She listens to me answer my daily questions, questions that I write and I answer, every day. Why do I do this? My name is Marshall Goldsmith. I'm too cowardly to do this by myself and too undisciplined. I need help, and it's okay!
>
> How about you? Where are some areas where you might need a little help? Make a checklist of behaviors and actions that you want to improve on and then ask someone to help you by listening to you gauge how you're doing every day. It's simple and still hard to do because we have to look at ourselves every single day. We give ourselves feedback every single day and we ask someone else to help us be accountable. It's a great tool." Marshall Goldsmith
>
> http://www.marshallgoldsmith.com/articles/the-greatest-threat-to-success-and-how-to-avoid-it/

You will get more from this relationship that you give. You may have read or heard that most people only retain 10% of what they read or hear; however, most will retain 90% of what they read or hear, put into practice, and then share and use to help others.

> If you find this information helpful. Please consider gifting a copy to a local jail or an organization that may benefit.

HABIT # 5

PLANNING

ONGOING AND REVISED AS OFTEN AS NEEDED

As the adage goes; "Fail to plan, plan to fail."

One of the huge downfalls of many practitioners of behavioral intervention is their inability or lack of understanding of the importance of recording and reviewing daily data, understanding what it is telling them, and appropriately adjusting the intervention as often as needed. I am not a fan of the music of **Jon Bon Jovi**, but I do love this quote: **"Map out your future --- but do it in pencil."** This demonstrates a clear understanding of one of the principle characteristics of success, being able to recognize the need to adjust, and knowing what adjustments to make.

While you may at times know you need to adjust, you may struggle to know what adjustments to make. That is one of the purposes of your support system, to include support groups; your personal data, The Foundation, and tools in this book. These can help you better understand where you need to adjust as you move forward with your plan. The Foundation will help you see your situation and understand your personal data more clearly.

. . . OK, we've already talked a lot about data. You keep data on what you eat and drink (calories in). You keep data on your exercise (calories out). You weigh yourself daily and keep data on weight loss and fluctuations. We've talked a lot about support. We will talk later about the skills, tools, and some additional resources. Now, we'll talk more about the importance of planning.

Planning is listed under habits because it's not something you do just once. As mentioned above, it is ongoing and must be adjusted as you move forward. For example: as I was losing the 115 pounds, things were going well. I had some ups and downs and plateaus, but mostly my weight was going down at a rather regular pace, then came THANKSGIVING. Some might have considered that Thanksgiving an abysmal failure. I over-ate, I ate things I should not have eaten, I messed up my blood sugar and I didn't feel well physically or mentally, for days. Within a few days, though, I was back on my old plan; but of course, what comes after Thanksgiving, CHRISTMAS! I knew I had to adjust my plan. I dropped all expectations of losing any weight over Christmas; I just wanted to make sure I didn't gain any. I also knew there would be overwhelming cues (temptations) during the holidays, food I would see and smell, people who would be eating delicious meats, potatoes, and deserts.

So... I adjusted my plan, which I'll explain later,

"I have not failed. I've just found 10,000 ways that won't work." - Thomas A. Edison and it worked. I turned failure into feedback. I turned bad days into good data.

Planning is individual. What worked for me, may not work for you and vice-versa.

This doesn't have to take a lot of time. Most of your plan will continue until you need to adjust. Start with your initial plan. Write it out below. This is just a draft. ALL your plans will just be drafts, until something comes along and you need to make another adjustment. Eventually, your plan will be fairly-solid, but even after about 7 years; I still need to make occasional adjustments due to changes and additional or new stresses in my life. Sometimes this may be removing a "gateway food" from my home. Sometimes it may mean making a new commitment with supportive people.

Write out your plan: (use a notebook for more space)

Write what you will eat in advance, perhaps even a week or more at a time. I usually record or at least plan my calories before I eat them. Recording my calories for the day in advance helps hold me to the plan because I don't want to have to change and reenter what I've eaten for the day. It helps reduce impulse eating because I've already decided on, planned, and recorded my meals for the day. In my case, I usually eat a big meal for breakfast now and I'm done for the day except for water and perhaps chewing gum (and I'm now trying to break the chewing gum habit). There is no way I could have done this when I started. My diabetes would not have allowed it and it would have been too difficult. When I first started, I ate three meals. I ate a large breakfast, a large lunch, a very small dinner, and sometimes a very small snack. Now it's easier to just eat the one meal a day and be done with it. That's me. May not be you. Remember: The Foundation, Habits, Skills, Tools, and Techniques are for everyone. Individual eating and exercise plans, are just that, individual. Some will have individual dietary needs due to health conditions. For most, these are only slight nuances or adjustments. For a few, the adjustments may be significant. We all have the same basic nutritional and exercise needs. Do the best you can according to your own situation and as mentioned numerous times, consult your physician.

Write out in advance how you will exercise. Remember, make gradual sustained progress, and don't try to overdo. Stand on a solid foundation. Just like with the old story of the tortoise and the hair, slow and steady really does win this race. Overdoing is just sabotaging yourself.

Write out contingency plans: what you will do in more difficult situations (the skills and tools portion will provide you with more information and ideas). Use your support system to brainstorm ideas that may help. If one thing doesn't work, then you've just discovered one thing that doesn't work for you, try another. A common feature of my diabetes prevention classes is having the class brainstorm ideas for each other.

Contingency plans do not need to be long and complicated. Keep them short and sweet. One short sentence is usually enough. Sometimes one word or even a picture is enough. Post your plans someplace easy to see and where they will be constant reminders... or cues. I have reminders in my office such as the exercise tubes and things I have written and put up on my wall. One of my current reminders and goals is related to finishing this edition of this book.

Here are a few examples of contingency plans:

1. At Christmas time, when I am really tempted to eat something delicious, and which is not in my planned meal, I will eat 20 salted peanuts instead. Remember these are all individual and this works for me, but may not work for you. We'll talk more about why I did this when we talk about skills and tools.
2. When going out for an early dinner (which is rare, but sometimes done for social reasons) or when having company over for dinner, when I have finished eating, I will push my chair back away from the table to about arm's length. This allows me to continue to be social while at the same time creating distance between me and the food which cuts down on "mindless eating" or "grazing". If possible, and there is a social reason to go out to eat, I prefer to go out for either breakfast or lunch when I am not as tired or stressed and have better control over my consumption. Additionally, ask for your plate to be removed, or if at home, remove it yourself then sit back down to chat. Make sure "grazing food" such as the bread basket are as far from you as possible. At a restaurant, you can also ask for a 'doggie bag" or 'to go" box and put half the food in the box, then put it to the side, even before you start eating. Currently, because of my commitment, if I go out to dinner, it must be an early dinner. For most restaurant chains and for restaurants you are familiar with, you can choose before you go. Choose wisely and stick with your choice.
3. When sick, (which is much rarer now, but still happens on occasion) I will reduce my caloric intake because I will be getting much less exercise.
4. When going to a potluck I will sit far away from the food. I will wait until everyone has gone through the line and then I will go through, if I go through at all. If I wait until the end, most of the high calorie food will already be gone. I will also make sure I take something healthy and

low calorie as my contribution.

These are individual for me and for my situation. As you write your plan and contingency plans, you will find that some work and some may not. You will need to continue to revise as often as necessary. Writing these out is more effective than just thinking them out. Writing helps you clarify your thoughts and helps put thought into action. Posting plans and goals in a place where you will see them regularly and where they will become reminders makes them more powerful. Having a calendar or something similar where you check off your success for a plan, goal, or objective, each day makes them even more powerful. You may find it helpful to rewrite your cues or reminders from time to time and even decorate or frame them in different ways so they continue to stand out and don't just fade into the background of things you don't really pay attention to any more. Remember, reminders can also be pictures, items, or collages. They can be something only you understand.

Your plan and contingency plans will probably not be the same and may not even be similar to others in your support group. Be very careful you do not try to impose what works for you, on others. Just as your plans must be individualized to your needs and situation, theirs must be individual for them. Support and help others in your support group (without dictating) to come up with their own plans based upon *The Foundation* plus these habits, skills, tools, and techniques. Such a group is a great way to brainstorm ideas for your individual plan and for your individual situation.

Remember, when writing plans if you record things you will not do, also record, focus on, and place an emphasis on, what you WILL do. Remember, you can get additional help on the Facebook page mentioned previously. . . If you wish.

This last Christmas, I gained a few pounds; but have since taken them off again. During Christmas, I ate more than usual; but now eat mostly healthy foods, but still slip just a little from time to time. You may not have to be perfect ALL the time. Some of you, because of your addiction, legal constraints, and/or medical condition, may need to be 100%. If you slip in any way, make sure you fail forward. Get up and move forward again. Admit and take responsibility for your mistakes, adjust, and turn bad days/nights, into good data.

Get help if needed, but move forward again.

"Success is the sum of small efforts, repeated day in and day out." – Robert Collier

Remember, plan, write your plan, and then practice following the plan.

"Be patient. Your skin took a while to deteriorate. Give it some time to reflect a calmer inner state. As one of my friends states on his Facebook profile: "The true Losers in Life, are not those who Try and Fail, but

These are helpful strategies for any addiction recovery.

> those who Fail to Try." — Jess C. Scott, Clear: A Guide to Treating Acne Naturally

These strategies can help you change longstanding and deeply entrenched habits.

Another great quote comes from a very good "B" movie, *Take Down*. **"Getting pinned is closer to victory than never getting on the mat at all."** It's a movie about a high school wrestling team and coach.

> "Will is a skill." — Jillian Michaels, Unlimited: A Three-Step Plan for Achieving Your Dreams

Next: Skills, Techniques, and Tools.

First another recipe:

This may sound a little strange but is surprisingly good and meets food security. As with all my smoothies, you can make it in the morning or the night before. If you make it the night before, just leave out the ice until morning. You can drink it all for breakfast or leave half for lunch. If you need something to chew on, try a couple pieces of whole wheat, oat, or brown rice toast.

In a blender

1 1/2 to 2 cups water

2 to 4 cups (packed) fresh (raw) spinach (anytime I include spinach in a smoothie, it's raw)

1 ripe avocado (seed and peel removed)

1 large (cored) apple (do not remove the peel, there is important nutrition there). I typically do not like Granny Smith Apples, but in this recipe, they are WONDERFUL!

1 tablespoon pumpkin pie spice

1 cup old fashioned rolled oats

1 cup milk (I prefer Almond)

1 scoop protein powder

1 teaspoon rosemary

Add stevia to taste

Blend well

> Add ice, a little at a time, blend. Continue to add ice until you have the desired consistency. (Remember, if this is too much for you, put part in the refrigerator and save until later.)

Section 3

AND NOW

THE FIVE SKILLS AND TOOLS

1

SET IN WRITING AND ACHIEVE REALISTIC GOALS

"The goal not written is merely a wish." Unknown

Fact: People who set and effectively write achievable goals are more likely to be successful than those who do not.

Before you write your goal, you need a great "**why**." If you don't have a great "why" then the best written goal and objectives won't matter one bit. It will just fade into the swamp and manure of unrealized goals common to the masses. Consider the following: there is a great deal of difference between an incentive and a reason. Make sure your "why" represents a <u>reason</u> you want to change. Most positive, lasting changes I have observed over the years working with people in the Diabetes Prevention Program and other areas of life and in counseling have been associated with a positive "why" which fell under one of these three categories: Health, Life, or Love. Incentives, such as new clothing, looking good for a vacation or wedding, are nice but generally do not last. No matter your addiction or the change you want to make, look for reasons associated with one or more of these: Health, Life, or Love. Think about your "why" in two parts. Write out why you want to achieve the goal and what the likely result will be if you do not. The positive why may be for yourself or for someone you care about. If you do want to get to a certain weight before a vacation or wedding, while this may be a great incentive, make sure you also have a good **reason**. Otherwise, once you have finished the vacation or other short-term incentive you're very likely to slip back into old habits. Perhaps you want to live to see your grandchildren or even great grandchildren grow up and enjoy doing things with them. What you want to avoid may be the loss of eyesight, the loss of a limb, dialysis, or early death. (For some addictions, it may be incarceration.) Perhaps you have a history of diabetes, heart disease, or cancer, in your family. In my case, it was all three plus Alzheimer's. Once you have identified your "why" and what you want to avoid. Write them down, create or find a picture, or make a collage that represents both your positive "why" and what you want to avoid, your default future. Put them both someplace where you will see them daily. From time to time, at least every three months, redo them so you remember and continue to notice them. Both your positive "why" and what you want to avoid may change over time, and that's ok. Your "whys" always need to be current, pertinent, and personally powerful.

I want to be clear, though. There is nothing wrong with short term incentives. We use them all the time and they can be powerful, but understand that moving to an important reason, a higher purpose, is always best. Let me share an example, in teaching children. You may need to provide an incentive to get a child to clean their room. Eventually by the time the child is an adult you hope they have a reason to keep their room and house clean without you providing short term incentives.

How to write a SMARTERR goal.

Specific (with a baseline)

Measurable

Achievable/**A**ttainable

Results-Focused

Time-Bound

Evaluate/Enhance/Adjust

Reporting/Accountability &

Reinforcement/Reward

When you write your goal(s), write a short term, long term, and mid-range goal. It's important you achieve a goal quickly. Make the short-term goal easy, the mid-range goal a little harder, and the long-term goal harder still (remember you may want to adjust as you collect data and learn about your individual situation, needs, and reaction, to the changes). It's important to achieve early success. This will build self-efficacy and help encourage you to continue. When I teach the Diabetes Prevention Program, no matter how much someone wants or needs to lose, the first goal is from 5% to 7%, no more. Once that has been achieved, the person who wants can set another achievable goal.

SMARTERR goals

Specific (with a baseline)**:**

Exactly what do you want to accomplish? Where do you want to go from here? In order to know where you want to go from here, you need to know where **here** is. That is your baseline, where you are starting from. If you need to lose weight or lose inches or stop drinking, you need an honest and accurate appraisal of where you are right now. What is your current weight? How many inches is your waistline now? How much of what, when, and with whom (if you drink alone, that is also important data), are you drinking now? (For binge drinkers or binge eaters that can vary widely and your starting point must reflect those fluctuations? The way you handle the fluctuations is to write your information over a period of time. For example: over one month I will eat about five to six thousand calories two to three times. On average, I will eat 2200 calories a day. As you can see, that tells a very different story than just saying you eat on average 2600 calories a day. Do you hide your drinking or eating? If yes, when and how and from whom?) What is your desired end weight? What is your desired end size?

Honesty is the first step in many 12 Step Programs. This includes being honest with yourself and others. Many addicts believe they are somehow hiding their addiction or the extent of their addiction and sometimes they can hide from some while it may be glaringly apparent to others. Honesty with self and at least a few others who will be both supportive and who will hold you accountable with carefrontation is essential. When I was morbidly obese and above 268 pounds at only 5'6" tall I would sometimes hide my binge eating. I was embarrassed. I wasn't fooling anyone. I ate too much and I was very fat.

Measurable:

Must be something easy to measure and while it can be in the negative; it must also have a positive component. For example: lose 50 lbs. Lose 1 lbs., per week for 50 weeks. (One to two pounds a week is a good solid, healthy goal.) Lose 8 inches around your waist. Walk one mile per day.

Share your goal(s) with a support person and double check to make sure their understanding of your written goal, what you are to accomplish, is the same as yours. (This is important because we sometimes believe something is measurable that either is not measurable or would be very difficult to measure.) Share with someone who, with carefrontation, will hold you accountable and provide you with honest and productive feedback. You must be mature and humble enough to allow them to do this without getting angry or jeopardizing the relationship even if they are awkward in their delivery and not as gracious as you might like.

Achievable/Attainable:

Do you have the tools, knowledge, and skills needed? If your goal is to not do something such as drink alcohol, view pornography, play internet games, etc., also include what you will replace it or these with.

Set goals which you have the power to attain or accomplish as YOU gain the skills and tools to help you achieve success. David McClelland was a psychologist who became famous for his work on "Need Theory". He is credited with developing what is referred to as "Achievement Motivation Theory" or "Need Achievement." People who are high need achievers set goals that stretch and require effort but are not too difficult to achieve. Basically, high need achievers are people who set goals which can be accomplished with effort and without excuses, even if adjustments are needed. Low need achievers are those who set goals which are so simple that they can rationalize that "anyone could have done it" and so don't ascribe any success to their own effort. Low need achievers are also people who set goals that are so difficult, they can rationalize that "no one could have done it." Low need achievers also purposely, perhaps even subconsciously, create situations where they can blame someone else when they do not reach their goals. Blame and rationalization are the hallmarks of low need achievers. Success, incremental success, feedback, and adjustment, are the hallmarks of high need achievers. High need achievers, are people who successfully reach goals, take responsibility and move forward after failure and/or amidst obstacles. Low need achievers rationalize and make excuses. High need achievers take responsibility and make changes. Low need achievers affix blame, often on others or situations, but sometimes even to themselves. Affixing blame is not the same as taking responsibility. Affixing blame usually does not result in any meaningful personal change, taking responsibility does. Taking responsibility requires personal change and improvement. Fixing blame does not. This is much like the difference between shame and guilt. Guilt, if managed properly can help you move forward and upward. Shame does not.

If you are, or sometimes are a low need achiever, you can change, you can

> This is such an important concept in writing your goals that if you do not understand this, please go to: http://weight-lossnewsandresearch.blogspot.com/2017/09/need-achievement.html for more information.

become a high need achiever. Doing the things discussed in this book will help you get started on this journey.

Results-Focused: Product over Process, Outcomes over Output

One of the first mistakes many people make when writing a goal or objectives, is confusing processes, with product, or output with outcomes. Process and output are what you do; product or outcomes are what you get, or the results of what you have done. The problem often occurs for people who confuse the two and think that because they do "A" they will get "B" and the two may not be connected. Some may think they **should** be connected but often there is no factual foundation for that belief. This is one of the reasons that a diet, any diet alone, rarely provides long term results. The person may be doing something, but they may not be doing the right things. Yes, they may lose weight and may even do it in a healthy way; but, without The Foundation, habits, and skills to maintain that weight loss, very few will obtain long term, healthy results. These changes in habits and the addition of skills, tools, and related knowledge, are really about lifestyle changes which in turn will change your life. How many times have you said to yourself or heard others say: I eat healthy but can't lose weight. It can be very easy to get very fat on very healthy foods, if your meals are not properly balanced, and you consume more calories than you use.

Establish a firm foundation and do the things which have been proven, to work long term.

Decide first on your desired outcome. Then make sure, according to both good research and your own personal data that your process is correct for the desired product or result. If you are not getting the results you want, you need to adjust your process. If you keep good data through an online calculator and the tools included here, you should have the information you need to move forward and achieve a healthier outcome. You will do much better with a coach and positive support such as in a recovery group or the diabetes prevention program.

> "There is nothing so useless as doing efficiently that which should not be done at all." - "Peter Drucker"

Time-Bound:

When will you accomplish this? If it is something ongoing such as avoiding something or maintaining a healthy lifestyle, set a specific time bound positive goals to coincide with the ongoing goal. You need to write specific times (dates) when you will accomplish your goal(s).

Evaluate/Enhance/Adjust:

Specifically, plan for: evaluation, enhancement, and adjustment. Include specific times, places, and support. This is usually best done with the support of someone who has gone before, someone who has accomplished what you want to accomplish. If you are a recovering alcoholic, get the support of someone who has been and is still successful in recovery. We all need positive mentors and role models, no matter our age.

About 30 years ago I had a friend who had made significant changes in his life and was a recovering alcoholic. He once told me there is nothing more annoying to an alcoholic than a recovering alcoholic. As a recovering food addict, I try not to be too annoying, but no matter your situation you need someone who will hold you accountable with appropriate carefrontation. Set specific times to meet with a mentor and/or group to evaluate and adjust. At first, you may need to do this daily, over time, weekly may be sufficient, but if you want to stay in recovery, you need to do this at least weekly. If your goal is related to weight and/or a food addiction, the Diabetes Prevention Program may be a good place to start. This individual or group must be able to lovingly hold you accountable. For some, this accountability may need to continue daily.

Remember: Failure is not the problem, we all fail. The key is to *Fail Forward*. Successful people learn to fail forward. The first step to failing forward is to identify and acknowledge your own mistakes, what did not work, and as much as possible (without dwelling on it too long), why it did not work. The second step is to recognize and sincerely acknowledge the success of others. (Remember: recognizing and acknowledging the success of others is an important element in developing **self**-efficacy.) Always: **Take Responsibility and Give Credit**. The third critical step is to, without boasting, recognize and acknowledge your own successes, no matter how small... and build on your own strengths and successes. The fourth is to make appropriate adjustments, and move forward.

Reporting/Accountability:

You must have someone who you can report to and who will lovingly but firmly hold you accountable. At first you need to communicate with this person on at least a weekly basis, or perhaps even daily. Even as you

> "I've missed more than 9,000 shots in my career. I've lost almost 300 games; 26 times, I've been trusted to take the game winning shot and missed. I've failed over and over and over again in my life. And that is why I succeed." — Michael Jordan
>
> Zig Ziglar, the famous motivational speaker has said: "If you learn from defeat, you haven't really lost."
>
> I tried and lost weight and gained it back again, then tried and failed repeatedly. Every time I learned something. I'm still learning and adjusting.

make good sustainable progress, depending on your goals/situation, you will continue to need this support. For some, group support will suffice. For some addictions, the price to pay for one slip is too high to ever let this accountability lapse. For some, you may need daily accountability the rest of your life. There are many extremely successful people in this world who include daily accountability based upon a personal list of important life skills. This takes only a few minutes a day but is one of their keys to their success. Marshall Goldsmith is a world-renowned business educator and coach. He has worked with many of the top executives in the world. He speaks to someone briefly, daily, who asks him a series of questions and he coaches others to do the same.
http://www.marshallgoldsmith.com/

> This book talks a lot about cues, influences, triggers, emotions, accomplices, friends, tools, habits, techniques, etc. Some can be positive and some

Reinforcement/Reward:

> negative. There are many things out there which can influence your choices. You <u>can</u> learn to "stack the deck" more in your favor. However; ultimately, you are responsible for your choices.

Celebrate success. It does not need to be expensive. Usually it is better if it is not. When losing weight, new clothing, even used, is a great way to celebrate. Be sure to donate old clothes that no longer fit as soon as possible. Get old clothing that is too large out of the house so you can't rationalize and think you can just go back to that clothing if you regain weight. If you are in another type of recovery, celebrate first your weeks of recovery, then your months of recovery, then your years of recovery in some small but significant manner for you. For something like annual recoveries, this may be a simple dinner (or breakfast) party or an annual hike or activity with friends and supporters.

Also, essential for successfully achieving goals and objectives:

> "There is no finer sensations in life that which comes with victory over one's self. Go forward to a goal of inward achievement, brushing aside all your old internal enemies as you advance." - Vash Young

Learn to be grateful. For some, this comes naturally, for others, it must be developed. Genuine gratitude, sincerely expressed, will help you achieve positive, productive, appropriate, goals. Really! Acknowledge the success in others, even when you slip yourself.

> "The only place you will find success before work is in the dictionary." Attributed to many people including Mary Smith and Vince Lombardi.

Remember, this can be hard work. Almost everything worthwhile is hard work, but it gets easier as it becomes habit. These new habits will become a part of the person you are becoming.

"The man (or woman) who wants a garden fair,

or small or very big,

With flowers growing here and there,

Must bend his (or her) back and dig.

The things are mighty few on earth,

That wishes can attain.

Whate'er we want of any worth,

We've got to work to gain.

It matters not what goal you seek,

Its secret here reposes:

You've got to dig from week to week,

To get Results or Roses."

Edgar A. Guest

Objectives: Goals are where you want to go. Objectives are the steps (or route) you will take to get there (goal).

A good objective will have four components: Who, What, When, and How.

Who: Who is going to do whatever. In almost all cases, this will be you. When you write out your objectives use your name or the word "I."

What: Exactly what are you going to do? Be as specific as possible without being too lengthy. You should be able to do this in one sentence.

When: When are you going to do this? You may need cues to remind you to do this. These could be Post-it notes. This cue could be a pair of running shoes on your chair in front of the television to remind you to take a run or walk before sitting down, etc. When may be, 'upon getting up in the morning,' or 'as soon as you get into the kitchen' etc.

How: How will you and others know you have completed the objective? If you are using an online calculator you will record it there. You will also report to your support system. This should be specific enough that others can easily recognize you have accomplished this objective. This must be written in terms which are easily measurable. For example, walking a mile or walking around the block is easily measurable; but, "taking a walk" is not as easily measurable. What exactly does it mean to "take a walk?" Does that mean you walked to the freezer to take the ice-cream out? Words like "feel," and "try," improve, and "behave," are also not measurable. Be sure your support system or mentor understands exactly what you are going to do, when you are going to do it, and how success will be measured.

All your goals will need at least one, and possibly many objectives. As you make progress, you may need to adjust your objectives until you have accomplished the goal. If your goal is to be able to hike a particular ten-mile trail close to where you live, you may need to set reasonable healthy objectives to work up to being able to accomplish that goal. I know I need to increase upper arm strength pulling down before I can climb to the top of the tower at the University of Idaho. I have added a specific exercise in my office, which I do briefly every day to help me accomplish this goal. My objective is to pull the resistance tube down 100 times every day at work. This objective will help me achieve the goal of climbing the tower.

Here's another example:

Objective: This morning for breakfast between 5:30 and 6:00 a.m. I will make and drink the Pina Colada Breakfast Shake/Smoothie.

In the above objective, I have included the *who*, "I" I have included the *what* (breakfast) I have included the *when* (the time and in this case the reminders or cues are my watch or clock) and I included the specific *how*, to the point that both I and others will be able to measure that I have accomplished my objective. (Sometimes the objective will need to be more specific and detailed than this example.)

Here is another example objective:

On Saturday morning, after I wake up and before 10:00 a.m. I will take Belle for a walk up the hill on the street where I live, past the eye clinic, down the trail to the west, through the trail by the medical building and back to my home.

Again, all four essential elements were included in the objective.

Use your support system for feedback on your goals and objectives.

Write at least one objective for each of your goals. If needed, write more and use additional paper.

FIVE MORE IMPORTANT ASSIGNMENTS FOR THIS CHAPTER

1. Write on a 3 x 5 card or use some other reminder, or cue to do the following every day: Write one personal success every day. No matter how small. Put in writing one thing you did right. Put that success someplace so it will be a reminder of something you did right or well. (If you wish, you can discard them after a week.)
2. If you haven't yet, watch the video about the Happy Secret mentioned previously. Take the "Gratitude Challenge."

Easy to read article: http://weight-

Doing this every day is very likely to improve your mood and even help you reduce stress. If you are at all a mood/stress eater, improving your mood will likely help you better control what you eat and drink, and control other aspects of your own life. In most cases it will also make you more pleasant to live with. Gratitude is also good for your health. . . And the psychological well-being of others around you.

lossnewsandresearch.blogspot.com/2014/11/thanksgiving-science-why-gratitude-is.html

Research:

Gratitude Toward God, Stress, and Health in Late Life

http://weight-lossnewsandresearch.blogspot.com/2018/01/gratitude-toward-god-stress-and-health.html

Counting blessings versus burdens: An experimental investigation of gratitude and subjective well-being in daily life.

http://weight-lossnewsandresearch.blogspot.com/2018/01/counting-blessings-versus-burdens.html

Gratitude as a Human Strength: Appraising the Evidence

http://weight-lossnewsandresearch.blogspot.com/2018/01/gratitude-as-human-strength-appraising.html

3. If you haven't yet, finish writing out your goals and get feedback from your support system. If you haven't found or developed a support system, ask people to help you. You may be surprised how many people really want to help and appreciate being asked for reasonable (but not overwhelming) help.
Make any additional adjustments you may need to make.

4. Be sure and finish writing out your plan after you have finished this book and have learned the other skills which will be covered.
Remember contingency plans. You'll learn more about what will be helpful later in this book and you can adjust; but, if you haven't yet, please start writing your plans.

James Abbott McNeill Whistler, the famous American born artist has been quoted to have said: "Hang on the walls of your mind the memory of your successes. Take counsel of your strength, not your weakness. Think of the good jobs you have done. Think of the times when you rose above your average level of performance and carried out an idea or a dream or a desire for which you had deeply longed. Hang these pictures on the walls of your mind and look at them as you travel the roadway of life."

"Every Worthy Act Is Difficult. Ascent Is Always Difficult. Descent Is Easy and Often Slippery" – Mahatma Gandhi

5. And **DO IT**! Revise as needed and remember we all fail. Learn to **fail forward**. Learn to turn failure into feedback and move forward.

I CHOOSE
HEALTH ~ LIFE ~ LOVE

What do you choose?

This is important; please write this down, something short and succinct.

"I choose: Health, Life, Love," is something I had on a sign on my wall for a long time. It is something I often remind myself. It is kind of a mantra. Another question I often ask myself when really tempted, is: "what is most important to me." While I occasionally slip, but much more rarely now, crap or poison is rarely more important for me than family and helping others.

"Though no one can go back and make a brand new start, anyone can start from now and make a brand new ending." Carl Bard

---

Before going on to the next three chapters I want to talk about DEADLY DOWNTIME.

I've talked about being more Reflective and less Reactive, at least until your reactions are much healthier. I've talked about how stress, fatigue, alcohol and many drugs will shift control from your cerebral cortex (thoughts) to your basil ganglia (habits). You must plan and practice specifically for these more difficult situations. Another big problem for many, is deadly downtime. This includes mindlessly watching television. The evenings when you are tired and/or stressed are especially difficult. Make sure you fill your time with <u>positive</u> activities you enjoy. We'll talk about what to do when/if you watch television in the next chapters.

Remember again, while motivation is important, even essential, it is not enough. You

> Take responsibility when it's yours, give credit where it's due.
>
> And remember: "People often say that motivation doesn't last. Neither does bathing that's why we recommend it daily." - Zig Ziggler

need The Foundation, plus sustainable skills, habits, and tools, to help you overcome any addiction. You also need an individual or a group to lovingly but firmly hold you accountable. At the very least, this must be weekly. For some it may need to be daily for the rest of your life. The question may come down to, is my success and health more important than immediate gratification, indulgence, intemperance, and pride? Yes, I am extremely redundant on extremely important matters.

2
AVOID

Close to where I live are many old windy roads creeping up and down mountain sides and down into and back out of valleys. Some of these roads used to be quite dangerous and frightening. Today, most have been replaced by better wider roads with fewer twists and turns. Perhaps you have been on or seen a picture of similar dangerous mountain roads.

There is an old story about a freight company that was hiring a driver to take the horses and wagons up such a road on a steep hillside to deliver the freight to the next town and return with another load. There were three people applying for the job. The first person took the team and wagon up the hill, back and forth through the switchbacks and across the prairie to the next town as quickly as possible for the driver. The second person believing it necessary to beat the time of the first driver took the turns on the steep and treacherous hillside even faster. Sometimes one or both outside wagon wheels would spin off the road and over the edge, the horses themselves barely staying on the twisting road.

The third person quickly took the road to the bottom of the hill, then slowed down while climbing up the treacherous grade. This driver hugged the inside of the road close to the inside of the hill, as far from the edge as possible. At the top of the hill, this person again picked up speed, delivered the freight then quickly returned to the dangerous grade where the wagon and team again slowed and carefully made their way back into the valley returning to the town and the freight office. This person's time was the slowest of the three.

Which person do you think got the job? Why?

The last person got the job. The person who AVOIDED the edge got the job. If you are a recovering alcoholic your goal is not to be able to enter a bar and not drink... your goal, the key almost always is to avoid those dangerous situations. This would include bars, and places where there is a lot of alcohol, and may even include friends and associates who drink.

It is the same with healthy or poor eating habits and foods you should not eat. The first key is to avoid. As with so many things in life:

The key is not just greater willpower...

The key is to avoid the edge.

Stay as far away from the edge as possible.

Don't just resist the temptation (cues), avoid the temptation!

If you have an overwhelming urge to stop at a particular store, restaurant, or stand where a particularly tempting food and/or beverage is served, and have not been able to resist the cues to stop, buy, and eat or drink, then drive or walk down a different street. While there may be new enticements, they may be easier to resist because stopping, buying, and eating/drinking in these new places are not engrained habits. It may be easier to pass the new temptations than the old ones, which because of ingrained habits and powerful cues are insurmountable <u>at this time</u>.

To the extent possible, avoid:

Difficult situations,

Difficult places,

Difficult smells,

And even. . . People who are not supportive of your goals and new habits. Even if you live with someone who is not supportive and who may even sabotage, if you cannot turn them from accomplice to a friend, spend less time with the accomplice and more time with friends. <u>In some situations, especially for addicts where there are legal ramifications</u>, you may have to create distance or even sever some relationships, at least for a time. Remember, your ability to help others is diminished until you are out of the swamp/manure and standing on firm ground.

What are some of the reasons someone might not be supportive? Think about it.

There are many reasons someone may not want to support you in your effort to change. "Misery Loves Company" is one possibility. They may be afraid you won't associate with them anymore if you change. They may be afraid you will give them a hard time and try to get them to change if you change and they do not. Remember: you can be supportive and encouraging in your change/journey without demeaning others. You can often have greater impact on the behavior of others simply by example without lecturing. If they ask a genuine question, provide only a brief, kind, answer unless they ask for more.

There may be people who have heard you say you have changed, or will change, many times before. They may have even seen you try to change and fail. Their expectations are that you will fail again. Expectations of others can be difficult to overcome. In the larger addiction recovery group my wife and I are involved with, one of the men recently mentioned the he is/was the "black sheep" of the family. When everyone else in the family treats you as the "black sheep" so to speak, it can be difficult to change. Personally, I prefer the story of the "Ugly Duckling" by Hans Christian Andersen. This story is our story. Most of us have been or are the "Ugly Duckling." In this story, an egg is somehow misplaced and added to a nest of duck eggs. When all the eggs hatch, there is one which is different and ugly in comparison to all the rest. This young bird is shunned and mistreated, but eventually grows into a beautiful swan. Sometimes when one person or child is a little different, that person is shunned and mistreated, though our potential, everyone's potential is beauty and greatness. Sometimes we try to hold someone down because we believe it will make us appear taller or better. Remember: **"You can't hold a man down without staying down with him;" Booker T Washington.** Booker T Washington had been a slave prior to The Civil War in the United States. He was an orator, educator, and the first leader of the Tuskegee Institute. He wrote an incredibly insightful book: *Up from Slavery*. This book is available to read on the internet.

Sometimes you can turn an accomplice (someone who helps you slide back into the manure or keeps you there with them) into a friend (someone who helps you get yourself out). How might you be able to turn someone who is unsupportive into someone who is supportive? You <u>may</u> find that some people who have not been supportive of your goals may become supportive if you have a conversation with them and ask them to help. Do not start by accusing them for anything in the past. Start with how you want to change your life and ask them if they might be willing to help and support you. You could honestly tell them you need and want help. Ask them if they have ideas on things they might do to help. This is generally much more effective than accusing them and telling them what you expect them to do differently. They may or may not have productive input, but usually it doesn't hurt to ask. If they do not want to be more supportive, don't press, just be a positive example and wait for possible genuine questions. (Even if this person will not, there are others just waiting and wanting to help.)

Granted: It is almost never possible to avoid all temptations and difficult situations. . . All the time. If it were, we probably wouldn't need any of the other skills.

There are some places, situations, and people, such as family, that may be difficult to avoid. However; if your addiction will get you into legal trouble and there are people who are not supportive of your efforts in recovery, avoid them.

There are some things now for me, which are not as tempting as they used to be. I can go into a deli and be around fried chicken and not crave the fried chicken. I have no cravings now for most candy. (Incidentally, I have had one exception to my "no candy" rule. On occasion, I have eaten small amounts of semi-sweet dark chocolate with fruit or nuts... and usually feel worse physically and mentally after I do. I have very recently decided it is time to put this aside too.)

When you are stressed, tired, or under the influence of drugs and/or alcohol, you will probably find you need to be even more strict about what you avoid. As mentioned previously, it is still better for me not to go grocery shopping in the evening or when I'm stressed because at those times I am more likely to do something I'll later regret. It is also unwise for me to go shopping without a specific written list.

What and possibly even who do you need to avoid, especially when stressed and/or tired?

Let me give you one more example to think about in relation to the wagon mentioned at the beginning of this chapter. If you were riding in the back of the wagon, on the tailgate at the very edge, and the wagon hit a bump, and you ended up in the pile of manure the wagon had just passed over, whose fault would that be??? You just never know when the wagon is going to hit a bump. Stay away from the edge. Stay as far away as possible from difficult situations.

AVOID
WHAT YOU CANNOT RESIST
OR HAVE DIFFICULTY RESISTING

To the greatest extent possible:

Do not buy it

Do not have it in your house (If someone else has it in the house, ask them to hide it and keep it out of sight. It is best if they support you and just don't have it in the house.)

NEVER have anything you do not want to over-eat or drink near you

Do not have it in your car

Do not have it at work (If someone else has it at work, ask that it be placed far away from you and out of sight. The more distance from you, the better for you.)

Avoid having anything even the least bit tempting you do not want to eat or drink within arm's length or eyesight.

Avoid it (whatever "IT" is)

While you can ask for the support of others, this is something you need to be assertive about, in a loving and kind manner. Remember, there are and will be those who may not want you to rise out of the swamp or manure. It is easier to look down upon, or to control others, or think better of yourself when there are others bogged down in a foot of manure even deeper than your own.

> "If you accept the expectations of others, especially negative ones, then you never will change the outcome." Michael Jordan
>
> "If you hear a voice within you say 'you cannot paint,' then by all means paint and that voice will be silenced." Vincent Van Gogh

One of the members of one of my Diabetes Prevention Program classes noticed that when she would go out to eat at a buffet or potluck, even if she sat as far away from the food as possible, if she had two drinks, it was like she was suddenly sitting right next to the buffet. This insight based upon her personal data caused her to make some adjustments. Because of her efforts and personal adjustments, she ended up losing 14% of her body weight. In her case, she learned she had to absolutely limit drinking to one drink. For many, the limit is none.

Here's another recipe: There is **a simple bean and brown rice dip** I make that my wife particularly loves.

Start with one cup brown rice. Add 4 cups of water and bring to a hard boil in a pan with a lid on top. Turn to low and allow it to simmer for 15 – 20 minutes.

In a frying pan sprayed with canned oil (I like to use cast iron, partially because of the benefit of the added iron.)

Add two large chopped onions

One cup chopped peppers (if you want it very mild then use bell peppers, if you want it hotter, banana peppers, if you want it hot, jalapeno peppers, or any combination)

One cup chopped tomatoes (green or tomatoes that are not completely ripe are best)

Sauté until mostly soft

Add the stalk of one piece of bok Choy cut into very small pieces with the bottom end cut off.

Sauté and stir, but only lightly sauté the bok Choy.

In a large casserole dish add two 14-16 oz. cans of refried beans

1 similar sized can of black beans, with the liquid

1 similar sized can of olives with the olives, sliced, add the liquid

Add the brown rice

Add the sautéed vegetables and the leafy top of the bok Choy cut into small pieces.

Add one similar sized can of diced tomatoes

Add one similar sized can of tomato sauce

Mix everything well and put into an oven preheated to 225 for 45 minutes.

Remove and add one pound of shredded mozzarella cheese. Mix well and place back in the oven for another 20 minutes. (The cheese is optional and can be omitted if you are vegan.)

Remove and serve hot.

This meets food security, has a complete protein, and has something from all food groups.

This is a very healthy meal, but the problem is the chips.

You want to find chips that are firm and not likely to break and are low fat and low sodium. Even with this, you want to limit the number of chips you eat. Enjoy.

Never assume you no longer need to avoid something, especially if it could lead to serious legal, ethical, health, or moral, difficulties. While I can now walk through a deli and smell fried food, not only without it, causing temptation but with a level of abhorrence, I understand that my addiction and binge eating for many things is only one bite away. My mother used to say something and I don't remember exactly what it was but it was something like one of the following three quotes:

"First, we abhor, then we ignore, then we embrace." "First, we tolerate, then we accept, then we embrace." "First, we abhor then we endure then we embrace."

I'm sure you get the idea. If you spend a lot of time around something you do not want to participate in or partake of, even if at that moment, you abhor it, you are risking embracing what you currently abhor.

There is a concept often discussed for alcoholics, or recovering alcoholics. When you are clean and sober you are you, the person you are, the real you. If you take one sip of alcohol, you become a completely different person. The rational person you may have been, is gone. The same can be said of a binge eater. While you must eat or consume nutrition in some way, if you take one bite when you are very tired or under a great deal of stress, you are a different person. Your addiction is now a compulsion. The rational, reflective person is gone, leaving only the irrational, reactive, reflexive aspect of yourself. All is not lost, but you have stacked the deck against yourself. It is similar for almost any addiction.

3
UNDERSTAND AND USE INCOMPATABLE BEHAVIORS

Incompatible Behavior is a basic concept of behavioral science. There are some behaviors which are completely or at least mostly incompatible with other behaviors. For example: I found a picture of a sign on the internet. The sign said:

SWIMMING NOTICE

MINNESOTA

STATE LAW

STRICTLY

PROHIBITS

UNDERWATER SMOKING

While not absolutely incompatible, the two are mostly incompatible and it would take quite a bit of effort and creativity to both swim underwater and smoke at the same time. (I have no idea if the sign was a spoof or not; but it is a great illustration of the concept.) Many years ago, I saw a poster, in a local Jr. High School, of a young person swimming underwater. The poster said: 'Research has proven it is very difficult to smoke marijuana while swimming under water.'

For me, an incompatible behavior or activity with eating is hiking with Belle. Belle is an energetic young white German Shepherd and while she is easy to walk, she demands my attention, especially when hiking. It would be very difficult to try to hold something and eat while hiking with her. Hiking alone requires extra exertion, but coupled with Belle it would be very difficult to eat at the same time. Other examples might be swimming, knitting, crocheting, sewing, galloping a horse, riding a motorcycle, or jumping rope.

Write down things you can do when you are tempted, which are incompatible with eating. Include these in your plan. When you cannot avoid something tempting, try doing an incompatible activity. When I was losing the 115 pounds and I would really feel an overwhelming desire to eat something accessible, I would go exercise, usually a long walk up a hill. This provided double benefit. Chewing gum is another commonly used and is mostly incompatible with eating. (Avoid gum with sugar.)

I am also at times a stress eater, in other words; one of my default behaviors when stressed was to eat. I still get urges/cravings when stressed. Eating seemed to provide some relief to my stress. (Part of the reason for this is that as children, many of us are/were programed to associate "comfort food" with stressful events.) Many of the incompatible behaviors I now employ provide much better stress relief than eating ever did. I am providing for an *underlying need* with a much healthier choice, such as exercise, to include taking a walk or hike with Belle. Walking with someone, talking, listening without judging or an angry reaction, can also provide much better and healthier outcomes in stressful situations. Remember, if you walk with someone, over time dialogue is more likely to emerge. Part of the reason for this is that walking, especially if it's brisk in the beginning, will help reduce stress and make it easier to communicate.

This was part of my plan; now add to your plan. What will you do? Remember, you may write something down that does not work as effectively as you would like at first. Run this by your support system and brainstorm. Your support group may be able to help you come up with other incompatible activities. Adjust your plan as you move forward, even if you fail forward.

What incompatible behaviors might you be able to use? Please write possible incompatible behaviors or activities you might engage in instead of eating.

Yes, this requires work, as does anything worthwhile. For almost everyone, it becomes easier and takes less time with practice.

"When everything seems to be going against you, remember that the airplane takes off against the wind, not with it." Henry Ford

4

UNDERSTAND AND USE ALTERNATIVE BEHAVIORS

Another basic concept of behavioral science is the use of *alternative behaviors* or activities.

When I was a boy, my dad bought me a Holstein calf from my uncle's dairy. I named her Babe. I would scratch and pet her, feed and water her. I cared for her, spent time with her, and I loved her. When I would go out into the pasture she would come running and stop right in front of me. She would start licking me, much like a dog might do.

One day I had entered the pasture with two of my friends. Babe saw me and started running towards me like she would do. Holstein's are big cows. My friends who interpreted the running more as charging, both ran as fast as they could to the fence and climbed over. Babe ran right to me, came to a sudden stop and started licking me, as I knew she would. My friends cautiously returned to the pasture.

Now that you have seen a picture of a Holstein cow and I've talked a bit about Babe, I would like you to do an experiment, a test if you will. Frankly, when I have done presentations, very few people have passed this test. For the next minute, I want you to *not* think of a cow or anything to do with a cow. You can't think of anything leather. You can't think of anything made from dairy. You can't think of anything made from meat. No stake, hamburger, cheese, or milk. Nothing associated with cows or cattle. Ok, time yourself and don't think of any of these things for the next minute. …

OK, how did you do? You may have had an advantage over most people when I've presented because this book has been full of clues. It is impossible to NOT think of a cow or anything associated with a cow, or cattle. BUT, it is possible to think of something else. Remember: Nature Abhors a Vacuum. You can **think** of something else and when you have addictive urges, you can DO something else. This may be an incompatible behavior as discussed in the previous chapter or it may be an alternative behavior as discussed in this chapter. Remember the quote mentioned previously and this is applicable to any addiction: 'It's more about crowding out than cutting out.'

I have already mentioned one alternative behavior I have used, salted peanuts. When I have been REALLY tempted to eat something with sugar, corn syrup, and/or lots of fats or any of the bad fats, I have used salted peanuts as an alternative food behavior. Fortunately, I have now trained myself to automatically respond to corn syrup and foods with a lot of sugar and even simple carbs such as pastries with the thought, "CRAP" and/or, "POISON" so it is no longer an issue, but for a while I used peanuts a lot and still do for other foods I'm trying to avoid or reduce consumption. Yes, you can still put on weight and you can still get too much salt/sodium from salted peanuts, but they are a better choice than the foods I am avoiding. I have also been able to limit the number, partially because when I do this, I get them in their shell and it takes me longer to remove the peanuts from the shell and eat them. This additional time helps me regain better control. Other shelled nuts have also worked in the same way and are often even healthier. When I have used the peanut alternative behavior, I record in my online calculator in advance that I will eat twenty. This helps me set the limit. If by the time I have finished the 20, I'm still feeling an overwhelming urge, I can record eating another 20, then count out another 20, then shell and eat each one. Fortunately, it is very rare that I need to do it twice. (I have done the same with almonds in the shell.)

Another alternative behavior which has worked well for me has been drinking non-caffeinated herbal teas. In the past, I didn't like these, but have grown to enjoy them. I no longer drink them as much as I did in the first year because I don't have as much need and I now rarely drink anything in the evening except water. Herbal teas have the added benefit of providing some nutrition while satisfying the need to eat or drink something.

Both nuts in a shell and peanuts provide for my underlying cravings with an alternative and healthier behavior. In this scenario, I am still eating or drinking something, but making a significantly better choice. Another option for me has been baby dill pickles. There is some good nutrition and they take as much energy to eat and digest as their calories, so the net calories is 0; however, they are high in sodium. Bread and Butter Pickles are not a good option. They are very high in calories and while delicious, to me, they fall more under the category of Crap. Because of my commitment to not eat in the evening or night, when needed, I use an incompatible behavior.

Write out foods you could eat or beverages you might drink, which though not perfect, might satisfy your need and be a better choice than the overwhelming temptation you are having difficulty avoiding. Again, use your support system to help you brainstorm different possibilities. If you have a doctor, dietician, or coach you are working with, run your alternative foods/beverages by this person to make sure they really are a better choice.

Do not use this as an excuse to overeat something a little healthier. You still must stay within your calorie budget. IF you go over, that means you must exercise more, but never use this for an excuse. Stay under your calorie and fat budget. If you are in a diabetes prevention program your coach will help you set a fat budget. If you do not have a good resource to help you set your fat budget, stay between 33 and 55 grams of fat per day.

If there are routines which have been associated with poor food choices, you might arrange for healthy food choices to be more available when you are involved with those routines. Eliminate access to poor choices or crap. For example, while watching TV if you MUST snack because it is such an ingrained habit, keep something close such as apples, celery, and baby dill pickles. You can also have nuts (not peanuts or pistachios) in their shell with a nut cracker close by. These can also be overeaten, but are better choices. Over time it is better for you to not associate eating with television.

Think of: Avoiding, Incompatible Behaviors/Activities, and Alternative Behaviors; as Good, Better, and Best. Avoiding is best whenever possible. When not possible, engage in an incompatible behavior or activity. When neither avoiding nor engaging in incompatible behaviors/activities are possible, use an alternative behavior such as making a limited and healthier but still satisfying food/drink choice. For me at Thanksgiving or Christmas, eating twenty salted peanuts is a much better choice than the pecan pie sitting on the table. Avoid, stay as far away as possible from the poor choices, or in other words, avoid the crap and poison. Air popped popcorn without salt, butter, or margarine may be an optional alternative behavior for some. Even lightly salted with less butter may be an option.

On occasion, I must admit I go to a "less poor" alternative behavior. For example, if I have a strong

> It is similar for almost any addiction. Avoid if possible, and when not possible, identify and engage in incompatible behaviors or alternative better behaviors.

urge for soda, I might have Wyler's no sugar drink. However, I understand an herbal tea is a better alternative choice, as is water.

Here are a few additional very simple recipes:

In a blender, add one peeled grapefruit.

Add 1 cup of water

Add 1 cup of ice

Add ½ cup stevia granules; adjust according to your taste.

Blend well and drink.

Here is another, and is especially delicious:

Add in a blender, two cups of frozen berries or fruit (unsweetened) of your choice

Add 1 cup almond (or other kind of) milk

Add ½ cup of stevia granules; adjust according to taste. This will vary widely depending on the fruit. Some fruit may not need any stevia.

What alternative foods/beverages can you try? This list will also need to be adjusted as you move forward. You may find some additional ideas here:
http://www.quickhealthymealsonabudget.blogspot.com/

Please write your possible alternative behaviors or choices below:

List of alternative foods you might consider adding to your list above, to try to curb or move past cravings:

Gum (of course not a food but for many does satisfy some underlying needs)

Baby dill pickles, Celery, Grapefruit, Lettuce, Nuts in shells, Air popped popcorn with low or no salt/butter (avoid margarine)

Steamed or fresh:

Broccoli, Cabbage, Cauliflower, (No dressing, dip, butter, etc.)

If you are a binge eater and it is in the evening or during the night, find something that will satisfy the urge without opening the door to continue to binge. In other words, don't eat or drink anything that will increase compulsion to eat or drink more. If needed, make a list of prohibited foods and drinks, adding to the list as necessary.

5

UNDERSTAND, BE AWARE OF, AND USE THE POWER OF CLASSICAL CONDITIONING And CUES

Some of you may remember the story about Pavlov and his dogs. Pavlov was the Russian scientist who discovered after ringing a bell to feed his dogs, that after this pairing of the sound of the bell with the food for a length of time; the dogs would salivate just from the sound of the bell. The dogs would do this even without the presence of the food. This led to the discovery of what we now call Classical Conditioning. For our purposes here, think of Classical Conditioning as those cues or triggers which occur in our environment and which create a physiological, chemical, and sometimes addictive response, such as an almost overwhelming desire to eat or drink a craved food or beverage. This can apply to almost any addiction or behavior, such as alcohol, gambling, online gaming, or using social media. These become habits you automatically respond to even without thinking.

When a child is upset and we give that child a piece of candy or cookie, or another food, just like Pavlov's dogs, that child comes to associate those comfort foods/crap, with any kind of stress. For the moment, they seem to provide some comfort, but like many drugs, alcohol, and other addictive behaviors, it can become an addictive cycle spiraling downward.

Some cues can be overwhelming. For example, think how much more of an urgent need you sometimes have when you must relieve yourself after a walk, drive, meeting, or class. Have you noticed the need seems more urgent as you finally leave that meeting or class, or as you are approaching a restroom? Environmental as well as contextual cues related to time and habit can be extremely powerful. If you are an alcoholic and walk into a bar, even if it's an empty bar with no one drinking, you are likely to experience powerful urges to drink. For some of you, just being in a kitchen, or opening the refrigerator may cause powerful urges to eat. If that is the case, avoid. In the case of the kitchen or refrigerator, while you may not be able to avoid all the time, you can possibly avoid those places in the afternoon or evening. If you are addicted to gambling or shopping, there may be places, people, or things, you need to avoid.

What are some of the CUES that create an almost irresistible urge for you to eat or drink something you should not? Please write these down. For me, one of the most difficult cues was the smell of fried chicken either in a deli or from a restaurant. Fortunately, after retraining myself, those smells, no longer have the same power over me. Though other things continue to be tempting, fried chicken and other deli smells are now easily ignored. As I am working on an edit of this book it is Halloween night 2017. My granddaughter has been here and we have a bowl full of candy. Most of it has no effect on me; however, I quickly rationalize the peanut M&Ms are at least, a little healthy. I quickly reframe it as crap and remind myself it's after 5: P.M., so poison again avoided. In the past, I may not have made as good a choice.

> What are the most difficult cues you need to avoid?

Understand that cues are more difficult to resist when under stress, tired, or under the influence of a drug or alcohol.

Avoid those cues when possible and PLAN for those cues when impossible to avoid. Over time it is possible to retrain yourself, just like Pavlov's dogs, to change your response to almost any cue. You can retrain yourself to the point that the smell or sight of something you now crave, cues, or reminds you to do something other than eat/drink. Often you can retrain yourself so the cue completely loses all power over you as I have done with the smells from the deli. If you associate some cues with the thought of poison and/or crap, over time, that is what will come to mind. My purpose in including some of the pictures earlier in the book and referring to manure multiple times has been to create an association for you between something disgusting, and unhealthy foods and habits. If after reading this book, when you look at a doughnut, you think of a pile of manure and are even a bit repulsed, that is helpful classical conditioning.

Through retraining yourself and developing new habits, a cue which used to coerce you to eat something, **can** remind you to do something different. This will work better if the new habit fills the same underlying need. For me, the underlying need has been quite often not hunger; but something else, often more emotional than physical. Over time I have found healthier ways to meet those needs. Quite often I needed more healthy ways to relieve stress. When the underlying need <u>was</u> hunger, I found alternative and healthier ways to meet my need for nourishment. You can too. You may even come to abhor that which you now embrace. You can also come to love and enjoy that which is healthy and helps you move forward and upwards.

Once you have identified those cues which now seem overwhelming, write a plan for each. Remember, first avoid, second use incompatible behaviors, third use alternative behaviors or foods.

If you change your grocery shopping habits to only shop with a list, when neither tired nor stressed, and avoid the more dangerous parts of the store, and you **still** find yourself buying unhealthy foods, try dislodging your old food buying habits. Try a new store where you are not in the habit of buying unhealthy foods and/or try shopping with a supportive friend. (Never shop with an accomplice.) Another strategy may be to order your food online and have it delivered or even asking a friend to order it for you. Remember, if the addiction can have legal ramifications and/or cause harm to you or someone else, you may need to always avoid those potential dangerous cues. Somethings are just not worth testing.

Cues **can also be** a powerful force to help you make positive choices. For example: cues in your natural environment during your typical routine can remind you. . . And almost compel you... to exercise, eat or drink something healthy, or follow your plan. This may take some time, but as you practice a new habit and develop a new reaction to an old overwhelming cue, you can retrain yourself to a new behavior based upon that same cue. Stress and pain are now more likely to compel me to walk with Belle than eat. Exercise tubes sitting on my desk at work remind me to do certain brief exercises during my work day. Other examples are the signs, pictures, posters, or collages you can put on your wall as reminders of both your healthy desires and goals as well as what you hope to avoid.

During a previous editing of this part of the book, I was feeling a little stressed. Many years ago, my reaction would have been to find something with sugar or simple carbohydrates, and eat. Now, my first reaction would typically be to take a walk with Belle (an incompatible activity), but sometimes that is not a good option. For a couple of years my second reaction or response to this cue would be to have some herbal tea (an alternative behavior). Now, those urges are completely gone.

As you create new habits, built around healthy cues, you will slowly change your life, develop more and better self-control, and create a healthier you.

Over time I have been able to reprogram my responses to visual and olfactory cues (smells). "Poison" is now my automatic reaction to many foods and drinks. While that may seem a bit extreme, it works for me and because of my diabetes, even though it is completely under control, these foods are poison for me. (One definition of poison is something that causes a disturbance or ill effect to your body.) Another change in response to a cue is: when I know I have eaten all I need nutritionally, and I get pangs of hunger, I have learned to enjoy the feeling. I consider it a success and source of accomplishment. I now realize it represents a greater level of self-control. These changes did not happen overnight. They took months, and in some cases a couple of years.

What are the cues in your natural routine/environment that you may need to avoid and/or change? Please write them out. You will likely identify more as you progress towards your goal of health. Remember, people can be cues too. For an alcohol or drug addict, there are people who will be cues for you to use. It is the same for many food addicts as well as other addictions. Just being in association with these people will create a strong urge to use or engage in the addiction. If you cannot quickly turn the accomplices into friends, make new friends. Create new more healthy associations. If some of these associations are close family members you do not want to completely avoid, carefully choose the types of activities and times for interactions.

What are positive cues in your natural environment/routine which you may want to strengthen or add to your environment/routine? These are the cues or reminders to do something positive towards your goal. Please write these out. These may be things like the exercise tubes on my desk at work, walking shoes on your favorite evening chair, and the dog leash next to the door. They may also be pictures of children, grandchildren, or someone doing a healthy activity you'd like to be able to do.

Positive cues to do things you want to do.

Remember, large companies and small businesses around the world have become expert with cues or enticements. (An enticement is another way to think of a cue, and sometimes for some of us, these enticements can become overwhelming.) Most of the time, no matter what is said about higher motivations, these companies or organizations are motivated to make money and/or gain power and influence. Even the best-intentioned companies, must have a profit motivation of some kind, otherwise they would no longer be in business and would no longer be able to pay employees and supply you with your wants or needs, at the lowest possible price. We are almost constantly bombarded with competing advertising or enticements. Not all enticements are bad and they do not all support evil intentions. One of the goals of this book has been to teach you to recognize the difference and to promote health, life, and love, for you, your family, friends, and colleagues. You can provide positive social and environmental incentives for others to make better choices. This is often best done without saying a word. When my wife and I were first married, I was interested in moving back to Idaho. My wife did not want to live in Idaho. I bought a calendar with beautiful pictures of Idaho and stopped talking about it. We moved for a few years to Washington and now live in Idaho.

Organizing your environment, reminders, and cues, will help you organize your life and make you more efficient.

Remember: Cues can be internal or external. Feelings (e.g. pain, hunger, strong emotions, or an urge to use the restroom), sight, sound, touch, smell, people, situations, events, seasons, time of day, holidays, etc. can all be cues which urge you to behave in certain ways according to your personal programing, which in many cases, you can change.

(Some strong emotional cues which may be negative and which you may need to overcome or learn to replace are: self-pity, pride, loneliness, sadness, anger, impatience, rejection, longing, abandonment, jalousie, and resentment. Yes, there are many others. Hopefully this book and the support groups mentioned will help you begin both your physical and emotional recovery. For those of you who will do an inventory as part of one of the 12 step programs, you may find the feelings that led to your behavior, are _almost_ as important as the behavior. Reinterpreting events that led to feelings, responding with more positive and productive feelings, while still holding others appropriately accountable, may help you change your reaction, keep you in the middle of the wagon, and from falling into the pile of manure below.)

PUTTING IT ALL TOGETHER

One of many things I have heard repeatedly from people in recovery is the realization that the addiction that got them into trouble and brought them to the group was only the surface of the problem. Once they began their journey in recovery in earnest, they discovered other addictions. One common discovered addiction was anger. Anger, according to Jerald Jampolsky, author of <u>Love Is Letting Go of Fear</u>, is simply a manifestation of fear. Perhaps **fear** is an addiction common to many of us: fear of failure, fear of success, fear of the unknown, fear of loneliness, fear of loss, fear of difference, fear of anything we don't understand, or with which we disagree, fear of whatever. Is it possible to be addicted to an emotion or a reaction? Is fear simply a habitual response?

For my purposes, it really doesn't matter. Fear is something that holds many of us back and keeps us from realizing our potential. The remedy for fear is faith. The replacement for fear, is faith. Alfred Bandura may call it self-efficacy, but sometimes refers to faith. In my personal research, the key ingredients of true faith are: Love, Truth, Works, and Humility. Love yourself and others, learn and understand the truth, do the hard work, and realize you may need to change the way you think and some of the things you do. Admit your mistakes, when you are wrong. Recognize when you need help. We all need help. Ask those to help you, who are in the best position to really help.

What fears do you have that may be keeping you from accomplishing your goal or making the change you wish to make?
How can you use Love, Truth, Work, and Humility to overcome these fears?

~~~

Remember, you need a support group, coach, and/or mentor. You may want to find a **Diabetes Prevention Program** close to where you live. There are also Addiction Recovery

Programs, mostly free or very low cost, which can help. Alcoholics Anonymous, Narcotics Anonymous, Overeaters Anonymous, TOPS, and Gamblers Anonymous, are just a few examples. Weight Watchers also has helped many. Many support programs have groups for spouses, family, and friends. The 12 Step Program has a great Spouse and Family Support Group. Support groups for spouses and friends can help members learn appropriate boundaries and healthy ways to provide support. They can also help family and friends heal from the damage often associated with chronic exposure to addiction.

These programs can help the addict and the family member develop new healthier habits. I hope this book will also help many.

> "We speak, it is true, of good habits and of bad habits; but, when people use the word 'habit,' in the majority of instances it is a bad habit which they have in mind. They talk of the smoking-habit and the swearing-habit and the drinking-habit, but not of the abstention-habit or the moderation-habit or the courage-habit. But the fact is that our virtues are habits as much as our vices". William James: *Talks to Teachers*: Chapter 8

Sticking to the same routines (where and when), using the same natural cues day after day, will help you establish new and healthy habits. When you move out of your new routines of; eating, sleep, exercise, work, etc., you will become more vulnerable to the old habits. These are also times when you will need to be extra vigilant and plan for situations.

This may seem like a lot of work, but anything worthwhile takes effort and as quoted previously, "the only place you will find success before work is in the dictionary." Over time, as these changes become habit and as you become accustomed to recording data and adjusting your plan, it will take less time, will become easier, and you will have more time and energy to do the things you enjoy and need to do.

I won't say: "good luck" because it's no more a matter of luck than it is solely a matter of motivation. **I will say: move forward,** even **fail forward. Achieve success!**

So, remember within your capacity, which is almost always far greater than you currently realize:

- **DAILY**

- **DECISIONS**

- **DETERMINE**

- **DESTINY**

As you begin, it may be that minute by minute decisions determine destiny. Over time it will not be as daunting or difficult. Daily, weekly, monthly, plans will become easier to make and follow. As you do this, your capacity will increase, perhaps more than you ever dreamed. Over time you will also find it easier and much less time consuming. As you take the road less traveled, don't take the journey alone, there are others; find others, who will take the journey with you.

APPENDIX

Additional Goal and Objectives Worksheet

Remember:

Goals are where you want to go.

Objectives are the steps you need to take to get there.

Goal:

Write one thing you would like to accomplish or be different in your life. Remember: this needs to be something important that will stretch you, not be too easy, and must be within your ability to accomplish (even if it requires you to gain some additional skills/tools). Make sure it is easily measurable and easily understood by others. . . Get feedback.

Remember: Specific (with a baseline), Measurable, Achievable/Attainable, Results-Focused, Time-Bound, Evaluate/Enhance/Adjust, Reporting/Accountability & Reinforcement/Reward

Write your goal below:

What is your current baseline? In relation to this goal, where are you starting from or what is your current status?

What is your Default Future if you do not achieve this goal? Sometimes a picture reminder may be helpful. Like the positive "why," change the picture periodically so you do not begin to overlook/ignore the picture. The positive "why" should be more prominent, but it is also important to keep what you want to avoid in the back of your mind.

By when do you plan to accomplish this goal? (Write a specific date)

What knowledge, skills, and tools, will you need to gain that you do not currently have to accomplish this goal? (Seek expert feedback to make sure you are seeking the correct skills, knowledge, and tools, to accomplish your goal.)

To whom or to what organization will you report progress on at least a weekly basis? (Be sure they are willing to support you by firmly but lovingly holding you accountable, using "carefrontation.")

How will you celebrate the accomplishment of your goal? (Spend no, or minimal money. You don't want your celebration to be bigger than the actual accomplishment of the goal.)

[ ]

Set a reminder such as a sign on your wall to write something positive you have done every day. If it pertains to this goal, that's even better, but it doesn't have to pertain to this goal. Just write one positive accomplishment every day.

Objectives:

Remember, these are the steps to accomplish the goal. Write who will do what, when and how you will know it's been achieved (criteria for success). Remember, it's always best if the **who is you**! That's the only person you can or should truly have control over. Remember to get feedback.

Who?

[ ]

What?

[ ]

When?

[ ]

Criteria for success:

[ ]

If progress is limited or nonexistent, are you taking the wrong steps [objectives] to achieve your goal? Consider the data, skills, tools, achievability, value, etc. Remember: **"There is nothing**

181

so useless as doing efficiently that which should not be done at all." Peter Drucker

To discuss or ask questions about goals or objectives you can go here:
http://goals4outcomes.blogspot.com/

<u>Begin</u> to behave like you are what you want to be.

CREATING A CALENDAR OR GOAL CHART

Use a simple monthly calendar.

Next to the calendar, post your plan (this can be a monthly or weekly plan, and if needed can even be a daily plan which you create some time the evening before or first thing in the morning).

For every day, you complete any one of the habits and/or reach a goal as planned, make a colored check mark on the calendar (use a different color for each habit and each goal), or place a small sticker (again a different sticker for each habit and each goal). Keep it simple, don't try to do too much at once.

Include in your plan what and when you will eat.

At what time each day will you will weigh yourself?

Include when and what you will do for exercise (and preferably with whom).

Who will you report to, when, and how?

When will you update your plan?

If you found this book helpful, please gift it forward to someone who can join you on your journey or someone you would like to help.

Data: Compare your food/beverage consumption and exercise with the following chart.

Rate how you feel from 0-5 with 0 being "like crap" and 5 being great.	Sunday	Monday	Tuesday	Wednesday	Thursday	Friday	Saturday
Record how clear your mind is from 0 - 5							
Weight							
Pain levels from 0 - 5							
If you have diabetes, what is blood sugar? If you record multiple times, record each.							
Make notes about what you did right or what you may need to avoid or do differently. If you over ate, or ate crap, what may have been negative cues or setting events (things that may have caused you extra fatigue or stress. If you did well, what might have helped?							

When you compare with your diet or what you have eaten, understand that you may feel the effects of what you eat for two or three days. If you are consistent with this, over time you will begin to see patterns. If you do not, while it's not a good idea to do this for a long time, eat the same thing for a few days in a row then just change or add one thing/food. That may make it easier for you to see a pattern.

There are always fluctuations in how you feel. Sometimes you feel better and sometimes you feel worse. Diet, exercise, emotional stresses, sleep, thinking, medications, drugs, alcohol, etc. can all have an impact. Do a personal data study to better learn what causes your fluctuations.

Bonus Tips:

I recently took a break from writing and took Belle for a long walk. The route I chose allowed her to run through a field, but also took us by a frozen yogurt place I really like and a smoke house that smelled delicious. I knew I didn't want to eat any more and took neither money nor plastic. I would have resisted the smoke house anyway, but perhaps not the yogurt. That kept me from purchasing. I know this tactic will not work for everyone and every addiction. For example: I am told that not having money is no real obstacle for an alcoholic.

Travel, Restaurants, Eating Out, Meal Time:

When eating out, avoid buffets. If you find yourself in a buffet, sit as far from the food as possible. Always take your time and eat slowly. Take your time to get to the food. Decide what you are going to eat in advance, not as you are passing by with your plate. If you do not know what is available, make a walk through and decide what your healthiest options are, then getting a plate and only add those items. Stay away from the foods you need to avoid. In restaurants, if eating alone, leave as soon as you are done. When with others, ask for your plate to be removed when you are done eating and move your chair back a little from the table. Move back enough so you cannot reach food such as bread, but remain close enough to be able to continue to socialize.

Salads are often a good option but avoid most dressings. You may want to try a vinaigrette. Fish without a lot of butter or cream sauce, vegetables, and fruit, are often good options. Remember: when possible use a small plate or saucer (what used to be considered a normal plate), ask for a doggie or "to go" bag and put extra food there.

One restaurant I have found to have good choices has been Panera Bread. https://www.panerabread.com/en-us/home.html/ I would not recommend everything but they have some good options. For fast food, I really like Jimmy John's #13 on whole wheat bread. https://www.jimmyjohns.com/ When I'm traveling, I want to make sure I get good nutrition and maintain The Foundation. At Subway, I have found the veggie delight on 9 grain wheat, with swiss or provolone an excellent option (I wish they had smoked Gouda). Someone who works at a Subway in Kellogg, Idaho recommended I have it toasted after the cheese and the vegetables have been added. It's delicious that way. I ask for all the vegetables except for jalapenos. If you like jalapenos, include them too. After it has been toasted, I ask for mustard and vinegar. It is delicious and quite nutritious. http://www.subway.com/en-us Another very nice option for a healthy drink with additional nutrition is Jamba Juice. http://www.jambajuice.com/#

Most Mongolian restaurants/grills are a good option. You can choose exactly what you want included and the sauce, or no sauce. Most have very low calorie and low-fat options for both food and sauce.

When eating at home or holding a dinner party, leave the food on the counter. Allow people to dish up at the counter and take their plate to the table. This will reduce grazing or mindless eating.

In the social sciences, we often speak of ***secondary gain***. Secondary gain refers to the rewards we may be getting from something that otherwise might seem bad. Examples may be someone who is frequently ill, but derives some satisfaction or alleviates fear through controlling others or having others take care of him or her. This can be as basic as the child who is sick, and may, in reality feel sick, because s/he is afraid of a test, or bullies at school. It can also refer to the proverbial "headache" someone may have when another wants them to do something. This does not mean the person is faking it. The distress at the thought of having to do something, can cause physical discomfort, pain, and help to lower the immune system creating more opportunity for illness. This is one of the reasons it is so important to learn to resolve, manage, avoid and in some extreme cases, escape from stressors and dangerous situations.

Sometimes, quite often really, secondary gains may get in the way of our success.

Are you sabotaging your own success? Obstacles that may be keeping you from success. No matter your goal or objective.

List 7 reasons you think your life might be worse if you achieve your goal and/or overcome your addiction.

Next logically respond to each. You may need the help of a supportive friend.

How might your reasons be faulty thinking OR how can you turn the negative into a positive?

Next, list 7 reasons your life will likely be better if you achieve your goal. Don't leave them here. Post for you to see or remember. One alternative way of posting is to put them on your computer so they automatically pop up each day when you login.

Daily Inventory:

There is benefit from this for anyone and there are many ways to do it. For a serious addict or someone who seriously wants to improve their life, this is crucial. Make a list of 10 to 20 behaviors and/or thoughts which are crucial for changes/improvements you want to make. These may be a combination of cues (things, smells, people, sounds, sights) you need to avoid, replacement behaviors, thoughts, and other behaviors or activities. Phrase them as questions. For example:

Have I been kind?

Have I stayed away from…?

Have I replaced negative thoughts with…? (There is no need to write out the negative because that will just remind you of that thought. List possible positive replacement thoughts, poems, or songs, you can use in these situations.)

Do this daily. It will be more effective if you report this to someone.

Additional questions that may help.

What am I doing that is helping or working?

What am I doing that is making things worse or keeping me from progressing?

How can I do more of the things that are working or helpful?

For many years of my life I had a dear friend and mentor. He, like my father had served in The Pacific, in the Navy during World War II. He and my father would often get together and tell funny stories and laugh about their experiences. I never heard my father talk of his tragic experiences in the war until he developed Alzheimer's, and then it was for only a brief period. I also never heard Frank talk about his tragic experiences, of which I'm sure he had many.

Frank hated zucchini. And as was characteristic of Frank and my father, he dealt with this strong abhorrence with humor. He liked to tell zucchini jokes. For example: Why did Henry Ford invent the pickup truck? To haul zucchini away. Why were locks invented for car doors? To keep friends and neighbors from filling your car with zucchini. One time I invited Frank and his family over for dinner. Everything; meatloaf, pies, jello-salad, stir fry, bread, was all made from zucchini. (In retrospect, I'm glad he wasn't allergic and I didn't poison anyone.) He thought it was funny or at least acted as if it were humorous. Anyway, this recipe is dedicated to Frank Clark.

Zucchinatouille

Add in this order, in a casserole dish. (Add each item evenly over the previously added item to create a layer.)

3 tablespoons olive oil

1 tablespoon roasted garlic or 3 cloves, sliced garlic

1 - 2 large chopped zucchini (or for options, you may use patty pan squash, yellow crooked or straight necked squash, or slightly immature butternut squash)

1 - 2 large bell pepper, chopped (or an equivalent amount of other types of peppers)

2 - 3 large tomatoes, cut into small pieces. (If you can get them, use green [not quite ripe] tomatoes.)

2 - 3 onions, chopped

1 cup sliced mushrooms

1 tablespoon oregano

1 tablespoon tarragon

(Optional) 1 tablespoon rosemary

1 cup dried cheese (for example, Parmesan)

Croutons - can be homemade from pieces of whole wheat bread, toasted and broken into small pieces

2 cans tomato soup (or two cans diced tomatoes is generally a healthier option.)

Bake at 350 for 45 minutes in a preheated oven

Foods that may help memory and feed the brain:

Avocados, Blueberries, Broccoli, Coconut Oil, Virgin Organic (In small amounts and not heated), Collard Greens, Grapes, Kale, Legumes, Salmon (wild is best)

Spinach, Sunflower Seeds, Turmeric, Walnuts, Whole grains

Scented Oils:

Scented oils which may help with weight loss – remember, for safety's sake, no fire. This is not something I know a lot about and do not have much experience with. I like scented oils and if you do and want to try some, try and see if it helps. If it's a pleasant scent you enjoy, then nothing lost. If it helps you lose weight, then added bonus.

Bergamot oil, Cinnamon oil, Fennel oil, Ginger oil, Grapefruit oil, Holy basil oil

Lavender oil, Lemon oil, Lemon grass oil, Juniper berry oil

For more information go to the link below and click on the link on the page there.

http://weight-lossnewsandresearch.blogspot.com/2017/08/essential-oils-and-weight-loss.html

There may be other better options, but most of the foods and health related products I purchase come from:

Grocery Outlet https://groceryoutlet.com/

Vitacost https://www.vitacost.com/

Walmart https://www.walmart.com/

Winco https://www.wincofoods.com/

I only mention this because I'm on a tight budget and you may be too. These are the places where I have so far, found the best prices. No, unfortunately I don't get any kickback for mentioning them.

Bonus Recipes:

Basic Brown Rice

Pour into a pot:

1 cup brown rice

3 cups water

Bring to a hard boil, then turn down to medium and allow to cook with a lid on until soft (about 15 minutes). Pour off any excess water. Add and stir in 1 tablespoon butter (not margarine), 1 teaspoon salt, 1 teaspoon cumin seeds. Enjoy.

Simple, Delicious Fried Potatoes

I do not recommend more than two or three potatoes a week. They are a very starchy food and some people with diabetes should avoid them all together. Pregnant women should also avoid potatoes because they may increase the risk of gestational diabetes.

Start with 1 or 2 clean potatoes. Leave the skin on and slice thinly. Put in the microwave. 1 minute for 1 potato, 2 for 2.

Using a non-calorie spray, butter flavored is best, spray a frying pan. (Cast iron is preferable.) Place the pan on the stove and turn the stove on medium high. When the pan is hot, put the thinly sliced potatoes in the pan. Turn occasionally to brown (but not burn) both sides until fully cooked. Put on plate. Add garlic and black pepper. Add Parmesan cheese. Enjoy.

Salmon Stack

Contains whole grains, protein, vegetables, fruit and some very healthy oils. Great for food security.

Mix in a food processor:

All the contents, including the water from a 5 oz. can Salmon. Or you can use 5 oz. fresh salmon either baked or broiled. If you use fresh salmon, use an additional 2 tablespoons of liquid from the jar of baby pickles to make a total of 4 tablespoons.

1 large stalk celery

4 baby dill pickles

1 avocado with the skin and seed removed

2 tablespoons olive oil or avocado mayonnaise

2 tablespoons of the liquid from the jar of baby pickles

Place between slices of whole grain bread. You will need from 4 to 6 pieces of bread. Makes 2-3 salmon stacks.

(Salmon Stack continued) Spray a frying pan (cast iron is best) with a butter flavored spray. Stove burner should be on medium. Place the sandwiches (stacks) on the frying pan, allow to fry for about two minutes or as you like it, then using a spatula turn the stacks and fry the other side. Serve warm. I think they are delicious.

Broccoli Salad

With mixer, mix

1 cup Greek yogurt (plain or vanilla with no sugar)

½ avocado (of course without the peel or seed)

Add to, and mix with spoon or fork

¼ cup chopped red onion

¼ cup raisins

1 head broccoli, cut into small pieces

1 ½ tbsp. Apple cider vinegar

¼ cup steel cut oats

¼ crushed walnuts

¼ cup pumpkin seeds

If you wish, you can lightly sauté the onion, walnuts, avocado, and cut broccoli, allow them to cool then mix with the other ingredients.

Chill in refrigerator and eat as desired

Brown Rice and Lentil Soup

1 cup brown rice

2 cups dried lentils

1/4 cup diced celery

2 cup chopped onion

1 teaspoon thyme

1 teaspoon rosemary

8 cups water

3/4 cup diced carrot

1 tablespoon salt

1 bay leaf

1 can water chestnuts (optional)

1/4 cup quinoa (optional)

2 1/2 cup diced tomatoes (from a can)

Rinse lentils and brown rice. Pour into a pot. Cover with 6 cups water. Put the lid on the pot.

Bring to boil.

Add 2 cups water and all ingredients except the tomatoes and bay leaf. Put the lid back on the pot.

Bring to boil.

Add tomatoes and bay leaf (and water chestnuts if desired). Put the lid back on the pot.

Bring to a boil, then turn to medium-low and allow to simmer for another 15 minutes.

Poor ~ Good ~ Better ~ Best, Table

Almost everything in the table below moves into the Poor/Crap category if not consumed in moderation. Obviously, this list is not complete. Just a little more to think about and something you may want to add to on your own.

Poor/Crap	Good	Better	Best
Yellow Cheese (Everything already listed as crap earlier in this book)	White Cheese	Swiss Cheese	Whole Grains i.e.
	Yogurt (some are better)	Gouda Cheese (For men, but in very small amounts. Gouda is a good source of vitamin K2, which is important for prostate health)	Wheat, Barley, Oats, Brown Rice. (If you are on a gluten free diet, oats and brown rice are a good option. Quinoa is also a good option, though technically a vegetable.)
		Parmesan (grated)	Nuts (in shells for snacking)
		Romano (grated)	Most vegetables and fruit
			Leafy vegetables, i.e. Spinach
			Avocados
			Berries
		Legumes	Apples
	Potatoes (avoid in any form if pregnant)		Grapes
	Corn		Pineapple

Go to the following link to learn more about the association of Gouda, Vitamin K2, and the Prostate (smoked Gouda, is my favorite).

http://weight-lossnewsandresearch.blogspot.com/2017/08/gouda-cheese-vitamin-k2-and-prostate.html

More Bonus Recipes:

Fruit Shake, alternate recipe:

In a blender, add 2 cups frozen fruit of your choice

1 cup milk, I prefer almond

½ cup stevia

1/8 cup quinoa

1/8 cup Chia seed

Or, in lieu of the quinoa and Chia seed, you can add ¼ cup steel cut oats.

My wife even loves this. Makes a delicious, nutritious, thick shake. This is sneaky nutrition.

Cauliflower Salad (Similar to potato salad)

Start with one large head of cauliflower. Remove the stem from the bottom. Break the florets apart and place in a pot. Cover with water and bring to a boil. As soon as it starts to boil. Turn the stove off and remove the pot from the burner. Allow to sit in the hot water for about 10 minutes, then remove the florets from the pot and place them in a large bowl.

Also, hard boil 3 large eggs and allow to cool. Best if you do this earlier so the hard-boiled eggs can cool in the refrigerator. After the eggs have cooled, remove the shell, slice the eggs, and place them into the bowl with the cauliflower.

Add:

½ cup chopped onions

1/3 chopped chives or green onion

2 tablespoon mustard (spicy brown if you want a bit of a bite to the taste)

¾ cup mayo (I prefer Kraft with olive oil)

¼ cup chopped olives

1 teaspoon salt

½ teaspoon cayenne (this is optional, adds some nice health benefits and more bite)

1 teaspoon paprika

1/3 cup chopped baby dill pickles

Baked Omelet:

This is simple, doesn't take long, and has something from every food group. You may want to wait to try this after you have become more accustomed to healthy food choices.

In a blender, add:

8 large eggs

1 ½ cup milk (Typically I prefer almond milk but dairy may be better in this recipe)

1 teaspoon salt

¼ teaspoon turmeric

¼ cup quinoa or Chia seed (This is an option but if you add it, you want to blend it well.)

Spray a large cookie sheet with spray oil

Pour mixture into the cookie sheet

Add and spread evenly

¼ cup chopped mushrooms

¼ cup chopped chives

¼ cup chopped tomatoes

¼ cup chopped olives

¼ cup chopped baby spinach

¼ cup mandarin oranges or pineapple (optional)

(You can alter the toppings as you wish, but this mixture is well balanced and has some great sneaky nutrition.)

Sprinkle on top ¼ cup grated Romano or Parmesan cheese

Put in oven preheated to 400 degrees for 15 minutes.

You can serve flat or rolled. Some may like catchup added.

This has a lot more eggs than I typically like to eat; however, the overall nutrition is great and there is at least something from every food group. Good way to start the day.

Unusual Healthy, Tasty Snacks (some may be high in fat and calories, but sure to count them all)

Asparagus, pickled

Brown rice: cook, then add salsa or hummus. Mix

Dill pickles, garlic

Garbanzo beans or chickpeas, baked in (cookie sheet) a film of olive oil with salt and one other spice, your choice… try something exotic… that you like or think you might like. Bake at about 450 until as crispy as you like.

Green olives stuffed with garlic and/or jalapeno (You can get them already stuffed in bottles at Walmart and probably many other stores… I'm not fond of green olives or jalapenos, but these are delicious.)

Crispy kale chips: Cut up kale into pieces a little larger than potato chips. Place on a cookie sheet in a thin film of olive oil. Add just a little salt. Bake at 400 until crisp.

Steak fries. Cut potato (sweet, russet, or red, are best) into long slices similar to French fries but about 3x thicker. Bake in (cookie sheet) about 1/8 inch of olive oil, at about 450 for about 45 minutes, then turn and continue baking until as crisp as you would like. You can add salt, but limit. Be careful about what, if anything, you dip them in. Simple ketchup, with little or no sugar or a mixture of tomato paste and apple cider vinegar may be an option. You may also want to try them with just a little salt and grated Parmesan or Romano cheese.

Trail mix. Make your own with nuts and dried fruit of your choice.

Zucchini: thinly sliced and baked until crispy in a film of olive oil. Covered with a light film of tomato sauce with just a touch of oregano and/or rosemary.

And for kids, start with: soft cream cheese, a no sugar added peanut butter, hummus, and/or salsa.

Put the items above (the glue) in bowls.

Provide plates or a cookie sheet for their work area. Provide plates of sliced nuts, vegetables and fruit. Let the kids create and eat what they want.

Herbs and Spices:

For any herb or spice, if you decide to use, use in moderation. Some herbs and spices can be very potent and can have serious negative side effects. There is much on the internet and in books on this subject, do your own research, consult with your physician or pharmacist about possible counter indications or interactions with medications. Never assume you can use an herb or spice instead of your medication. Never assume an herb or spice will solve your problem without doing other necessary things such as establishing the foundation daily. Never stop a medication against medical advice. Never diagnosis yourself from something you read on the internet or in a book. Consult a licensed physician.

Herbs and spices can add a great deal of flavor to your foods and in many cases, added health benefits. Some of my favorites are:

There are hundreds of great herbs and spices and many have potential health benefits. Don't expect any to cure anything. Just because an herb or spice provides some benefit to one person does not mean it will for you. We are all individual with individual constitutions. Do not overuse. Many can become toxic with overuse. I once had a woman with prediabetes in

Cayenne

http://weight-lossnewsandresearch.blogspot.com/2017/09/cayenne-pain-and-inflamation.html

Cinnamon

http://weight-lossnewsandresearch.blogspot.com/2017/09/cinnamon-and-t2-diabetes.html

Cumin

http://weight-lossnewsandresearch.blogspot.com/2017/09/cumin-and-cancer.html

http://weight-lossnewsandresearch.blogspot.com/2017/09/cumin-benefits.html

Garlic

http://weight-lossnewsandresearch.blogspot.com/2017/09/benefits-of-garlic.html

Licorice (Limit licorice. As with many herbs and spices there can be significant side effects in large quantities.)

http://weight-lossnewsandresearch.blogspot.com/2017/09/licorice.html

Rosemary

http://weight-lossnewsandresearch.blogspot.com/2017/09/rosemary.html

Tarragon

http://weight-lossnewsandresearch.blogspot.com/2017/09/health-benefits-of-tarragon.html

Turmeric

http://weight-lossnewsandresearch.blogspot.com/2017/08/turmeric-and-cancer_28.html

one of my classes who said she didn't understand why she was having problems with her blood sugar level because she was eating cinnamon. Unfortunately, most of the rest of her diet was crap and she didn't get much exercise. Even if it wasn't toxic in large doses, which it is, and she was to eat a mountain of cinnamon, it would not make up for other poor choices and habits. Neither will any herbs or spices for other conditions. It is the same with diet products, they will do little long-term good if you still have one leg in manure.

You simply cannot have one foot in addiction and the other in sobriety. Neither can you have one foot in health and the other in addiction. One foot or two feet, will stink all the same.

Foods, Herbs, and Spices, that MAY help alleviate pain.

Some herbs and spices are very potent. If you are taking medications, consult your pharmacist about possible interactions. If something seems to help, don't "go crazy" with it. Use in moderation. Usually just a teaspoon of the herbs and spices added to a prepared meal is plenty. For many of these, they can be added to a simple health stir-fry. Everything should be consumed in moderation and you need to rotate your diet to get a wide variety of nutrients.

Blueberries, Broccoli, Cardamom, Cherries (tart), Cinnamon, Chili Peppers, Cayenne,

Cloves, Cumin, Garlic, Ginger, Grapes (red), Marjoram, Mint, Mustard, Olive Oil, Oregano, Parsley, Pumpkin Seeds, Rosemary, Sage, Salmon, Sardines, Thyme, Turmeric

(Reduce consumption of anything with legs or wings.)

Foods, Herbs, and Spices, that MAY help reduce blood pressure. Remember: Moderation in all things.

Arugula, Basil, Beet greens, Beets, Berries, Cardamom, Cayenne, Cinnamon, Collard greens,

Curcumin, Flaxseed, Garlic, Ginger, Kale, Mackerel, Oats, Pomegranates, Romaine lettuce,

Salmon, Seeds, Spinach, Swiss chard, Turnip greens

Additional Addiction Resources

http://weight-lossnewsandresearch.blogspot.com/2017/10/cannabis-and-psychosis.html

http://weight-lossnewsandresearch.blogspot.com/2017/10/addiction-recovery-dog-therapy.html

http://weight-lossnewsandresearch.blogspot.com/2017/10/hippotherapy-and-addicton-recovery.html

http://weight-lossnewsandresearch.blogspot.com/2017/10/addiction-recovery-with-horses.html

http://weight-lossnewsandresearch.blogspot.com/2017/10/opioid-addiction-recovery.html

http://weight-lossnewsandresearch.blogspot.com/2017/10/opioid-addiction-symptoms.html

More on personal responsibility:

"Focusing on rights as the basis of conduct and policy is to create a society that is driven by advocacy, leading to a loss of community and reducing the motivation to work for the common good. ...

Gandhi spent more than 50 years in active public service and understood the need for legal safeguards to protect fundamental rights. However, he believed that a commitment to personal responsibility, not insistence on rights, should govern conduct and social policy.

H.G. Wells once asked for Gandhi's views on a document Wells had co-authored entitled Rights of Man. Gandhi did not agree with the documents emphasis on rights. He responded with a cable that said, I suggest the right way. "Begin with a charter of Duties of Man and I promise the rights will follow as spring follows winter."

Gandhi asked us to remember that if our rights are inalienable, our responsibility is indisputable - given to us by every religion and culture - to treat others as ourselves. He focused on this most fundamental of human responsibilities. If we keep it as our ideal and try to move toward it, we reduce the emphasis on rights and bring personal responsibility to a higher level in guiding our thoughts and actions. In both the political and business arenas, commitment to responsibilities impacts individuals and groups to look for ways to produce benefits for all. ...

There are pragmatic reasons for all of us to focus on our responsibilities rather than our rights. A society driven by the former promotes service, tolerance, compromise, and progress, whereas a society driven by the latter is preoccupied with acquisition, confrontation, and advocacy. ...

Gandhi took the concept one step further. He insisted that those being denied their rights also had to meet their responsibilities. Opponents were entitled to be treated as he would like to be treated - with courtesy and respect.

Even in the most intense phases of the struggles against the British, Gandhi was always respectful and courteous to the British as individuals. He sent then-Princess Elizabeth a wedding present - a tablecloth fashioned from yarn he had personally spun. He never forgot the human relationship in the political struggle. In today's political environment, we see an escalation of personal attacks at all levels, creating a climate of animosity and distrust and making it difficult to work for the common good. ...

He encouraged families to spin and weave cloth when they were not working in the fields. Doing work was their duty. He asked the rest of Indian society to live up to its end by giving up the more refined mill-made cloth and wearing the coarser hand-woven, hand-spun cloth made by the farmers as a way of helping them raise their economic status. Both parties were fulfilling their responsibilities; none were insisting on their rights.

Focusing on responsibilities removes the mind-set of giving something without return and of taking something without making a contribution. Both these attitudes are detrimental to the human spirit and create a society that is neither productive nor caring. The concept of meeting obligations because it is the right thing to do seems to be declining. We need to reverse this trend. When we direct our attention to our responsibilities, we are forced to look inward and ask what contribution can we make to create something better.

When Gandhi was asked about his message, he responded, my life is my message. This is true for each one of us - whether we like it or not - our life is our message. Meeting our responsibilities should be a way of life, not of gaining rewards. It should have its foundation in the family, where parents and elders are an example for their children, the leaders of the future.

Looking at the world through the lens of personal responsibility creates a landscape of hard work, high standards, commitment to service, and compassion." From: *A CLUE FROM GANDHI* by Kesavan Nair: <u>A Higher Standard of Leadership: Lessons from the Life of Gandhi</u> Paperback – January 1, 1997 by Keshavan Nair

"The concept of disease is fast replacing the concept of responsibility. With increasing zeal Americans use and interpret the assertion "I am sick" as equivalent to the assertion "I am not responsible": Smokers say they are not responsible for smoking, drinkers that they are not responsible for drinking, gamblers that they are not responsible for gambling, and mothers who murder their infants that they are not responsible for killing. To prove their point — and to capitalize on their self-destructive and destructive behavior — smokers, drinkers, gamblers, and insanity acquitees are suing tobacco companies, liquor companies, gambling casinos, and physicians." — Thomas Szasz

MORE BONUS RECIPES

Blueberry Maple Syrup Smoothie (Another smoothie that may help memory and cognition.)

This is another one of my shakes that may look and sound insane, but it's pretty-dang good and healthy for most.

If you have diabetes and want to try this, as with all my smoothies, make the smoothie but try only one cup. Test yourself about 10 minutes after and again an hour after. See how you feel. Maple Syrup has a relatively low glycemic index and this smoothie includes protein and whole grains and you may be able to tolerate it well, but should test yourself. Of course, follow your doctor's advice.

Maple Syrup is specifically used, along with Blueberries, Rolled Oats or Rolled Barley, and Turmeric because of their reported benefits for helping to delay Alzheimer's or possibly help keep it from developing at all. Please don't start drinking maple syrup straight out of the bottle. While there may be some benefits and it is a natural sweetener, this smoothie should be an occasional meal or treat and not frequent.

In a blender, add:

One cup hot water

2 cups blueberries (frozen)

1/4 cup maple syrup (this is real natural maple syrup, not the substitute)

1 cup rolled barley or rolled oats (if you are gluten intolerant, make sure you have gluten free rolled oats)

3 large carrots (I wash and cut off the ends)

1 scoop protein (depending on your individual needs, either pea protein or whey protein is recommended)

1 cup milk (I prefer almond)

1/2 teaspoon turmeric

Blend

Slowly add ice and blend until you have your desired consistency.

You can drink some, put in the fridge, then blend again and drink more later.

Simple, Healthy Crepe

Add to a blender:

2 cups old fashioned rolled oats

2 cups milk (I prefer Almond milk)

2 large eggs

1 tablespoon olive or avocado oil

Blend well

Pour part of the mixture into a nonstick crepe or frying pan

Carefully move the pan so the mixture covers the bottom and part of the sides of the pan. Turn over when bottom is done and cook the other side until it moves easily in the pan. Place on a large plate.

Add fruit. You can blend fresh fruit and if you wish, you can add just a little water and/or stevia in the blending or you can use something like Smucker's Simply Fruit.

Roll into crepe. (Makes 2-3 crepes.)

Gluten Free Pizza

Most pizzas falls under the poor/crap category. Depending on your choices, these fall under the good or better categories.

Add in a blender:

1 tablespoon olive oil

3 large eggs

3 cups rolled oats (if you need it to be gluten free, you will want to make sure the oats are certified gluten free)

3 cups fat free milk (you can also use a milk substitute such as almond milk or soy milk)

Blend well.

Poor into cookie sheets or round pizza pans.

Place in oven preheated to 400 degrees from 12 to 16 minutes.

Remove and allow cooling.

Add pasta sauce, then your favorite toppings with an emphasis on vegetable toppings, olives, and pineapple. Add

¼ -1/2 cup grated Romano or Parmesan cheese.

Put back in the oven at 300 degrees for 10 minutes.

-

For fruit pizza or combination fruit and vegetable pizza, make the crust as described above:

Add in a food processor:

1 tablespoon lemon juice

2/3 cup stevia

8 oz. non-fat cream cheese

32 oz. plain yogurt

Mix well

Pour onto cooked, but cooled pizza dough.

Cut up and add fruit to the top and if you wish, you may want to add some cut vegetables such as water chestnuts and chives.

Ready to eat and delicious.

Beat & Spinach Wilted Salad

Cut off the beet root from one whole beat which includes the stems and greens. Wash the root and put in covered pot and bring to a hard boil for 20 minutes. Allow to cool. Cut off the top and bottom ends and peel the very outside. Slice and cut the remaining beat into small pieces.

In a large frying pan, add 1/8 cup of either olive or avocado oil. Turn frying pan to medium heat.

Add the beet pieces and stir for sautéing.

Add one large chopped onion (peeled) and stir for sautéing.

Add one cup washed and chopped mushrooms. Stir.

Add 1/8 cup apple cider vinegar.

Add the stems of the beets, cut into small pieces. Stir.

Add ¼ cup Chia seeds and ¼ cup quinoa. Stir.

In a bowl, add 2 packed cups of washed spinach and the washed tops (greens) of the beats.

Add the hot sautéed mixture to the fresh spinach and beet greens and stir. This will cause the spinach and greens to wilt.

Add 1 cup well rinsed mandarin oranges. Stir. Enjoy.

Broiled Salmon

Spray the bottom of a pan. This can be a frying pan that you can put in the oven or a cookie sheet or a pan, specifically for broiling. Cover completely with butter flavored spray.

Place a piece of fresh salmon with the skin down on the pan.

Generously sprinkle lemon juice on the top of the salmon.

Lightly sprinkle black pepper and powdered garlic.

Cover with parsley flakes.

Broil for about 12 minutes.

I prefer to remove the salmon from the skin. Belle gets the skin and we get the salmon. Delicious and healthy. Some markets will have the freshest salmon in one place for three and then place it in another place for two more days at a substantially reduced price. Freshly caught is best.

Reframing cues (learning to respond in a healthier way) to cues and triggers that have in the past, prompted unhealthy/unhelpful choices or behaviors). Accompanied by a written plan for specific cues, with an old thought and new thought. Example. Smell of cinnamon roll, change from "I want" to "It's more important for me to live, be healthy, and enjoy my life and/or grandchildren." Or perhaps something more blunt as I have done: "That's crap." Or "That's poison." ☺ Or the question I often ask myself: "What's more important to me?" Write current cues you may have difficult with. This could be a sight, smell, person, sound, or anything that may compel you to do something you want to stop.	Write your response or thought you want to plant in your mind when you experience this cue.	Write what you will do, instead of what you have done in the past. For example, you may decide to take a different route and not go past a restaurant or store, you have difficulty with not stopping and eating what you should not. If you do go past the store or restaurant... or perhaps the plate of cookies in the office, what will you do instead of taking a cookie.
Cues or triggers (Write on next page)	Response in your mind.	What you will do differently.

Food that MAY help asthma: apples, avocados, berries, cantaloupe, carrots, garlic, leafy green vegetables, pumpkin seeds, salmon, spinach, tomatoes.

Foods that MAY make it worse: cheese, eggs, peanuts (yes, I'm cutting back or eliminating peanuts), salt (you must have some salt to live, talk with your physician or dietitian about what you need minimally), shellfish, crap to include wine.

As with all recommended foods, try adding or eliminating one food at a time for about a week to see if it makes a difference.

How am I doing? In personal transformation.	Rate from 0 – 4 (The purpose of this is to see how you are doing in individual areas. It is to help you see areas where you are doing well. Where you may need improvement and areas where you may need additional help.)	Rate yourself from 0 to 4 in each area.
Pertaining to your desired change: Do you have a reason, incentive, and fear (default future) posted where you can see it every day?	Rate 0 - 4	
Have eliminated, or do not eat "crap" or unhealthy food items.	0 Represents eating mostly unhealthy foods and beverages. 4 Represents all healthy food and beverage choices.	
Meet "food security" on a daily basis.	0 Represents never or less than weekly. 4 Represents every day.	
Have someone or a group I report to on a weekly basis (can be by phone) and who, with carefrontation, holds me accountable.	0 No, 4 Yes	
Manage stress well. No one or almost no one is stress free. Are you currently managing your stress well? If you rate yourself a 0 or 1 you may want to consider seeking help from a professional counselor. (Stress in and of itself may not be bad. Stress is often what helps us move forward, upward and to a better place. Sometimes it can be completely overwhelming, or even deadly. I hope yours is neither of these. If it is, please seek immediate help from the appropriate resource; your physician, law enforcement, a local hospital. If they are not the appropriate resource, they can guide you in the right direction. Most of the time and for most stress, most of us can do one of the following. Resolve it. Manage it. Let it go. I hope yours is one of these last three. I hope you	0 Represents not at all. 4 Represents, stress is well managed.	

make the best choice and have the skills to more forward accordingly. If you do not have the skills and need to gain them, you may want to consider seeking the help of a licensed professional counselor. Someone who can help you develop the skills to better manage moderate and minor stresses.		
Get between 7 and 9 hours of restful sleep per night. You may want to consult with your physician if you gave yourself a 0 or 1. There may be other reasons for getting too much or not getting enough sleep and you may also need to seek other help. For example, if your child is keeping you from sleeping, you may need to consult the child's physician and/or a behaviorist.	0 Represents less than one night per week. 4 Represents every night.	
Exercise aerobically 20+ minutes at least 5 days a week. If you are unable to do this at all, consult with your physician regarding healthy, safe, options. (Taking a walk counts. Remember to work up to this gradually if needed.)	0 Represents not at all or less than once per week. 4 Represents, yes.	
Eat a well-balanced, healthy breakfast.	0 Represents not at all or less than once per week. 4 Represents daily or on average 6 or more days per week.	
Good, positive social support. If you rate yourself 0 or 1, make connections and if needed seek assistance.	0 Represents none at all. 4 Represents, yes.	
Reframing cues (learning to respond in a healthier way) to cues and triggers that have in the past, prompted unhealthy/unhelpful choices or behaviors). Accompanied by a written plan for specific cues, with an old thought and new thought.	0 No written plan. 4 I have a written plan	
Have a written plan for better health. (Habit 5)	0 No, 4 Yes	
Have a written goal for better health.	0 No, 4 Yes	
Have a written plan to avoid difficult cues and triggers.	0 No, 4 Yes	
Have a written plan for possible incompatible	0 No, 4 Yes	

behaviors or choices.		
Have a positive/productive hobby you can and do engage in and which is an alternate to your addiction or compulsion and which helps reduce stress. If not, you may want to consider developing or getting help developing this. Do this in an area of interest to you.	0 No, 4 Yes	
Have a written plan for possible alternative behaviors or choices.	0 No, 4 Yes	
Have a positive/productive activity which helps others, involves others, and is an alternative to your addiction or compulsion. It is best if this activity is incompatible with your addiction or compulsion. If you are not involved with such an activity, on at least a monthly basis. You may want to develop this. Get help if needed.	0 No, 4 Yes	
Have a written plan to increase positive cues (reminders) in my life.	0 No, 4 Yes	
Have had a physical from my, or a, physician within the past year.	0 No, 4 Yes	
Am following the medical advice of my physician.	0 No, 4 Yes	

Self-talk/thoughts	
Discouraging and disabling (Write things that you may think or say to yourself which are discouraging.)	Encouraging and enabling (Write things you can say and perhaps post on your wall that will encourage you. One of my favorite for really-tough times is: If I still want it in the morning, I can eat it in the morning. 99.99% of the time, I no longer want it in the morning.)

Dark Chocolate Peanut Butter Cups

Turn stove to medium

Add to saucepan on stove, stirring until everything is melted and smooth

1 part dark chocolate squares (no sugar added)

1 part virgin organic coconut oil

1 part stevia (you may wish to adjust the combination a little differently according to your personal taste)

Spray a muffin tin/pan with butter flavored spray oil.

Pour chocolate mix to about 1/3 full

Add natural, no sugar, peanut butter

Pour chocolate mix on top to fill.

Chill in refrigerator

Here's a **holiday mix**. Not as healthy and not something I would choose to eat because of all the sugar, but for someone who is transitioning off sugar or a child who is accustomed to a lot of sugar and you want them to at least get some nutrition, this may be an option.

Pour into a bowl a box of Chex or Cheerios cereal.

Add dried fruit, such as mango and papaya, cut into small pieces, and/or raisins, cranberries, and banana chips.

Add dark chocolate covered nuts and berries.

Mix

Gluten Free Cobbler

In a blender, add:

3 cups rolled oats

3 cups milk (yes, I prefer almond)

3 large eggs

1 tbsp. Olive oil

Blend well.

In a rectangular cake pan spray with oil (I prefer butter flavored)

Pour the ingredients blended above and use a spatula to clean out the blender into the cake pan.

Using the blender again, add:

4 cups fruit, ½ cup stevia - Blend well

Pour evenly across the top of the batter in the pan.

Place pan into an oven preheated to 350 degrees and bake for about 35 minutes. Use a knife to test for it being done.

I Choose

Health – Life – Love

THE END

Well, almost the end.

You may have heard the term, "get around to it," or "it's time to get around to it." Well, now you have one. And now that you have one... just DO IT. (Yes, more of my odd humor.)

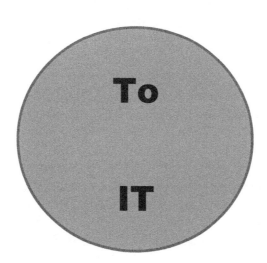

BONUS QUOTES

"Everything in our background has prepared us to know and resist a prison when the gates begin to close around us . . . But what if there are no cries of anguish to be heard? Who is prepared to take arms against a sea of amusements? To whom do we complain, and when, and in what tone of voice, when serious discourse dissolves into giggles? What is the antidote to a culture's being drained by laughter?" ― Neil Postman, Amusing Ourselves to Death

"Weight (too much or too little) is a by-product. Weight is what happens when you use food to flatten your life. Even with aching joints, it's not about food. Even with arthritis, diabetes, high blood pressure. It's about your desire to flatten your life. It's about the fact that you've given up without saying so. It's about your belief that it's not possible to live any other way -- and you're using food to act that out without ever having to admit it. (p. 53)" ― Geneen Roth, Women, Food and God: An Unexpected Path to Almost Everything

"Americans no longer talk to each other, they entertain each other. They do not exchange ideas, they exchange images. They do not argue with propositions; they argue with good looks, celebrities and commercials." ― Neil Postman, Amusing Ourselves to Death

"The only thing you sometimes have control over is perspective. You don't have control over your situation. But you have a choice about how you view it." - Chris Pine

"When a population becomes distracted by trivia, when cultural life is redefined as a perpetual round of entertainments, when serious public conversation becomes a form of baby-talk, when, in short, a people become an audience, and their public business a vaudeville act, then a nation finds itself at risk; culture-death is a clear possibility." ― Neil Postman, Amusing Ourselves to Death

"Anger ... it's a paralyzing emotion ... you can't get anything done. People sort of think it's an interesting, passionate, and igniting feeling — I don't think it's any of that — it's helpless ... it's absence of control — and I need all of my skills, all of the control, all of my powers ... and anger doesn't provide any of that — I have no use for it whatsoever." ― Toni Morrison

"I have three precious things which I hold fast and prize. The first is gentleness; the second is frugality; the third is humility, which keeps me from putting myself before others. Be gentle and you can be bold; be frugal and you can be liberal; avoid putting yourself before others and you can become a leader among men." ― Lao Tzu

"There is no dignity quite so impressive, and no independence quite so important, as living within your means." - Calvin Coolidge

"The way to wealth is as plain as the way to market. It depends chiefly on two words, industry and frugality: that is, waste neither time nor money, but make the best use of both. Without industry and frugality nothing will do, and with them everything." ― Benjamin Franklin

"He who will not economize will have to agonize" ― Confucius

Another Bonus Recipe
Bean and Brown Rice Dip
Another dish that helps provide food security. Something from every food group.

In a pot, add 1 ½ cup brown rice. Add 4 cups water. Put lid on pot and put on stove on high. Time from when you have a hard boil and allow to boil for 15 minutes. Stir occasionally.

Add to a large casserole dish or rectangular cake pan. Include any excess water.

Everything else you can do in a food processor.

Finely chop 1 ½ cups peppers. Your choice will have a big impact on the taste. I just made this and used one large jalapeno and one sweet bell pepper. Add to the casserole dish.

Finely chop 2 ½ cups onion. This will also have an impact on the taste. This time I used one very large yellow onion.

Add two 14.5 oz. cans of tomatoes. You can choose what you want. This time I used one can of diced tomatoes and one can of stewed tomatoes with Italian herbs. Put these also into the food processor and chop finely. Include the liquid. Add to the casserole dish.

Add one can olives, with the liquid, to the food processor and chop finely.

Add 3 16 oz. cans of beans. You can use whatever kind of beans, but will probably like refried beans best. You can add these with the olives and mix in the food processor. That will make it easier to mix with the other ingredients in the casserole dish. Add to the casserole dish and mix everything. (This time I used one can refried beans, one can black beans and one can garbanzo beans, with the liquid, finely chopped in the food processor.)

Put the casserole dish into an oven preheated to 400 degrees for 20 minutes.

Remove and stir in 1 lb. Mozzarella cheese. This time I used a mozzarella made from skim milk. I also shredded this in the food processor, but you can purchase and use shredded cheese.

Put back in the oven at the same temperature for another 20 minutes.

Take out, allow to cool a bit, and enjoy. I often eat this without chips. If you use a corn chip for dipping, use the healthiest you can find.

Tofu Mushroom Curry (meets *food security*) I hate tofu and I used to hate curry. I really like this. My wife also hates tofu and she kind-of likes this. Because of all the international students in our home over the years, we have often had Japanese students living with us or visiting. Many made great curry. I had had curry from other countries and not liked it. This has a milder taste. Two young ladies who did not live with us, but often visited and sometimes cooked in our home, were from Japan. One was from Fujisawa. She attends university in Tokyo. The other is from Tokyo. They both studied at Lewis-Clark State College in the U.S. They made especially delicious curry. This recipe is dedicated to these two wonderful, lovely, young ladies from Japan, **Yui and Yuki**. It is not the same as theirs, it is a combination of Japanese curry, Indian Curry, and a few additional alterations to meet food security, and make it more insanely healthy but still delicious.

Start with 3 cups water and 1 cup brown rice in a pot with a lid. Turn stove on high. Bring to a hard boil. Allow to boil for 15 minutes, then remove from the stove (stir occasionally). Add the cooked brown rice to a large pot (or you can just start with a large pot). Turn stove on medium high for this pot.

In a frying pan, pour a thin film of olive oil. Turn stove on high. Add about 2 ½ cups hard tofu, cut into about ½ inch pieces. Stir and turn until browned on all or most sides.

Add to the brown rice:
In order:
1 14.5 oz can vegetable broth
1 14.5 oz can tomatoes
1 cup water
1 cup coconut milk
Browned tofu cubes
Stir between each ingredient.
About 2 ½ cups finely chopped onion
About 2 ½ cups finely chopped potatoes (wash, but leave the skin on for the nutrition)
About ¼ cup finely chopped pepper (you can choose the type of pepper, I used sweet)
8 green onions (remove the very ends where the roots are and wash well). Cut into small pieces
2 large apples, washed, cored, finely chopped, with the skin still on (also for the nutrition)
About 1 cup not yet cooked green beans. Wash, remove the very end on both ends and cut in half
About 2 cups sliced mushrooms
2 green cardamom pods
½ cup vegetable flakes
2 tablespoons soy sauce
1 ½ teaspoon curry powder
1 teaspoon coriander or coriander seed
1 teaspoon turmeric
1 teaspoon cumin seeds
1 teaspoon ginger
Allow to boil for about 10 more minutes, stirring periodically. Make sure vegetables are soft but not mushy.

Lentil Soup (My wife really likes this. Does not quite meet food security.)
Turn stove on high.
Add to pot
1 14.5 oz can vegetable broth
2 cups water
Bring to hard boil
Stir between ingredients
Add 1 cup dried lentils
1 14.5 oz can tomatoes
About 2 ½ cups finely chopped red onions
8 green onions, remove the very end where the roots are, wash, cut into small pieces
1 clove garlic, chopped
¼ cup chopped onion (Your choice of the kind of pepper and your choice can make a substantial difference for the taste, if you want it milder, use a sweet onion, if you want it hot and spicy, use jalapeno. Or, you can use something in-between.)
Turn to low and allow to simmer until lentils and vegetables are soft but not mushy.

Recipe – **Jasmine's Swiss Chard**
- 2 Tbsp olive oil
- 2 bunches Swiss Chard coarsely chopped
- 1 cup chicken or vegetable broth
- 2 Shallots, finely chopped
- 3 garlic cloves
- 3 sweet mini peppers
- ½ Can black olives
- 1 can Garbanzo Beans, rinsed and drained
- Sea Salt to taste
- Pepper to taste
- Turmeric to taste
- Salt to taste
- 2 Tbsp Chia Seeds
- 2 Cups Brown rice cooked

1. In a large skillet, heat 2Tbsp of the olive oil over medium-high heat. Add the shallots, garlic, mini pepper, and the stems of the chard and cook, stirring until they are softened, about 2 minutes.

2. Add the chard leaves, Garbanzo beans, olives cook until chard is slightly wilted, 2 minutes. Add chicken broth and cover the skillet and cook for another 5 minutes.

3. Add salt, pepper, turmeric to taste.

4. Place mixture over brown rice and sprinkle Seeds before serving.

I've mentioned a facebook page located here:
https://www.facebook.com/DeliciousNutritionStealthHealth/
a few times. I post a lot of health-related information on this page. The primary topics are: diabetes, diet and weight-loss, Alzheimer's, autism, cancer, and some general health information. If you would like to be able to always see these posts when you log into facebook, go to the page, like the page, then and click on "Following." Then under "In Your News Feed," click on: "see first."

Conclusion:

I love the game Othello. I used to use it as a metaphor working with young people in counseling. If you understand and correctly apply the principles, even if you appear to be losing, you will almost always win in the end. I have not played much in years, but recently played with one of my very bright adult children. As we were playing he was asking questions about strategy and I was teaching. At a couple points during the game I thought he would likely win, but that was fine, because either way, it was a win for me.

> You may also be interested in the books: Autism (ASD) Intervention: The Very Basics, and Writing Contextually Mediated Measurable Behavioral Objectives (MBOs), for additional understanding of behavioral change.

Made in the USA
Monee, IL
05 November 2022

17175021R00122